IMPRESSIONS OF MEN AND MOVEMENTS AT THE UNIVERSITY OF NORTH CAROLINA

IMPRESSIONS

OF MEN AND MOVEMENTS
AT THE UNIVERSITY OF
NORTH CAROLINA — By
HENRY McGILBERT WAGSTAFF
Professor of History, 1907-45 Edited with
a Prefatory Note by LOUIS R. WILSON

THE UNIVERSITY OF NORTH
CAROLINA PRESS — *Chapel Hill*

Copyright, 1950, by
THE UNIVERSITY OF NORTH CAROLINA PRESS
PRINTED BY THE WILLIAM BYRD PRESS, INC.
Richmond, Virginia

PREFATORY NOTE

IN 1941 HENRY MCGILBERT WAGSTAFF, graduate of the Class of 1899 and Professor of History in the University of North Carolina, 1907-45, was requested by President Frank P. Graham to set down in permanent form his impressions of the University from the beginning until 1930.

The six chapters that constitute this manuscript are the result of this request. During the period from 1941 until his sudden death on May 28th 1945, Dr. Wagstaff spent considerable time in gathering materials concerning the University, reviewing its activities, and developing outlines and writing sketches of various periods of its history.

At the time of his death he had advanced his work to the point that he had prepared in penciled long-hand a connected first draft dealing with the historical background of the University, its establishment and its development from the beginning, through the periods of the Civil War, Reconstruction, and reopening, until the close of the administration of President Francis Preston Venable. Fragmentary sketches of the administrations of Presidents Edward Kidder Graham and Harry Woodburn Chase and comments on the Faculty of 1941 were also included in his papers, but they were so incomplete and disconnected that they could not be reduced to consecutive, intelligible typescript.

The seven chapters into which the papers have been more or less arbitrarily divided are as follows: Chapter I, Historical Background; the Administrations of Caldwell and Swain; Chapter II, the University under Reconstruction; Mrs. Spencer and the Reopening; Chapter III, The Selection of a President, Kemp Plummer Battle; Chapter IV, The Administration of Kemp Plummer Battle; Chapter V, The Administration of George Tayloe Winston; Chapter VI, The Administration of Edwin Anderson Alderman; and Chapter VII, The Administration of Francis Preston Venable.

In addition to telling the story of the founding and development of the University, Dr. Wagstaff skillfully traced the history of the educational, sectarian, and political influences that affected the University under Caldwell, Chapman, Swain, Battle, Winston, Alderman, and Venable. He likewise sketched with unusual penetration and charm the personalities of the presidents, of Mrs. Cornelia Phillips Spencer, and of a half dozen or more of the members of the Faculty who served under Presidents Winston, Alderman, and Venable.

The sketches in no sense present a complete history of the University for the periods covered. They were not intended to by their author, but they reflect the author's grasp of the social, political, and sectarian movements in North Carolina for a century and a quarter and the manner in which the successive presidents directed the University in its relation to them. He was altogether familiar with the interplay of Federalist-Whig ideas in the early period; the violent conflict of convictions during the Civil War and Reconstruction; the agrarian and sectarian movements of the 1880's and 1890's; and the upsurge of interest in elementary and secondary education and the education of women from 1880 to 1910. His knowledge of these ideas and movements, as well as of Presidents Battle, Winston, Alderman, and Venable as individuals with whom he had worked as student or colleague, was such as to enable him to comment upon them with discrimination and understanding. His characterization of the presidents and faculty members whom he knew personally are skillfully drawn and give interest and distinction to the story as a whole.

The manuscript falls short of being a complete history in another respect. The chapter on the administration of President Alderman, for example, seems to break off abruptly at the end of a paragraph that might well be thought of as being in the middle rather than at the end of the chapter. Several important developments which occurred during this administration are not included. Among these are the establishment of the School of Pharmacy in 1897 and the further development of the Department of Education in that year. The University was opened to women in 1898 and plans for the Alumni Building and the Carr Building were developed within the period. In fact the history had been developed at Dr. Wagstaff's death only to the point of being reduced to penciled longhand on note paper. It had not been typed or subjected to revision for publication nor had it been, as other of Dr. Wagstaff's papers had been, subjected to his own skillful polishing when seen in typed form or to the objective criticism of colleagues. Nevertheless it sets forth with unusual clarity and charm the impressions and keen insights of a mature, trained historian who had known the University for fifty years and was familiar with all the influences that had shaped it from its Revolutionary beginnings to its transition to a modern national university.

Chapel Hill, N. C.　　　　　　　　　　　　　　Louis R. Wilson
June 1, 1950

CONTENTS

	PAGE
Prefatory Note	v
1. Historical Background; The Administrations of Caldwell and Swain	3
2. The University under Reconstruction; Mrs. Spencer and the Reopening	15
3. The Selection of a President: Kemp Plummer Battle	23
4. The Administration of Kemp Plummer Battle	34
5. The Administration of George Tayloe Winston	51
6. The Administration of Edwin Anderson Alderman	66
7. The Administration of Francis Preston Venable	77
Index	105

IMPRESSIONS OF MEN AND MOVEMENTS AT THE
UNIVERSITY OF NORTH CAROLINA

1
HISTORICAL BACKGROUND; THE ADMINISTRATIONS OF CALDWELL AND SWAIN

THE UNIVERSITY OF NORTH CAROLINA from its chartering in 1789 to its temporary closing in 1871 was not a university in the widest sense of that term. Nor was it so in the early years after its reopening in 1875-76. Yet during that period it had an interesting life. It bore the seeds that were slowly germinating. This germination could not be faster than the condition of soil and climate dictated.

North Carolina as a British colony had been among the least promising. Socially, its population, sprung from various sources, lacked cohesion first of all in a geographical sense. Geography either tends to divide or unite. If the latter, then a corporate sense is soon created which lays the foundations for social unity. But with the birth of the Republic and North Carolina's emergence into statehood, these political events had operated merely to give an impetus to social and economic self-consciousness. Political self-consciousness outran both in further development, pushed by forces that gradually became common to all the members of the Union.

Colonial North Carolina, primarily a frontier area through its whole history, lacking in social and economic integration, had generated no effective demand for educational facilities provided by political authority, or much interest in such facilities provided by any other source or existing elsewhere. Political authority, i.e., government, in Old World colony-founding states was yet far distant from the period in which it was to assume any responsibility for popular education. The idea had not yet been born in Europe itself. For classes, of course, the state in some sense became a mild patron of education in the Middle Ages. But in general the institutional need had been left to private philanthropy and to the church. Explanation lies in the fact that government was yet universally class government.

In the British colonies founded in America in the seventeenth century, interest in facilities for education must needs wait not only on successful material development but on the development of a stronger cultural impluse in the Old World from which the colonies sprang. True, there was a mild deference for learning, popular and official, disclosed in the New England colonies and, to a lesser degree, southward. In the first area the explanation doubtless lay in the feeling of danger the Puritans had in respect to social and political isolation arising out of disinterest on the part of the British State as to their welfare. Also there was a feeling inherent in Calvinistic theology that to survive and perpetuate itself it would be necessary to arm itself with weapons of the intellect. In the colonies southward the impulse was milder still and, where appearing, grew out of two different sources. The first of these was a weak sense of missionary responsibility of the Church of England; the second—and this in a vague sense can be called class and official—the conviction that colonies were but extensions of the national territory and ought to have the same cultural opportunities as the home State.

Even so, the colony of North Carolina during the whole period of its political dependence, remaining socially and economically unintegrated, put little or no emphasis, popular or official, upon machinery for cultural advancement. The ground lay fallow. If here and there a merchant or a shipper in the few coastal plain villages—Wilmington, New Bern, Edenton, or Halifax, grew prosperous enough to further the cultural advantages of a son, he followed the pattern that has been stereotyped in British crown colony history. That is, he sent the son to England, as much with the view of enhancing the repute of a successful Englishman overseas as for satisfying a cultural demand. And such sons, after attaining some English education and contacts, often became the home representative of the colonial trader's business.

When in the last half of the eighteenth century political revolution, based fundamentally upon economic grievances, swept the American colonies along to a successful fight for independence, the colony of North Carolina was guided into and through the movement by merchant and trader interests. When the movement had arrived at climax, a spirit of near nationalism had been engendered in North Carolina. The dim vision of an independent North Carolina begat consideration of the future. A state without some evidence of cultural machinery would be but a poor state indeed. The merchants, traders, and the few prosperous planters who had made up the spearhead of the Revolution in North Carolina and were in complete command of the forming Revolutionary government, wrote into the State Constitution of 1776 (Section 41) that all useful learning shall be duly encouraged and promoted in one or more universities. Any articulation of this purpose must naturally have waited on the outcome of the general political movement of the associated colonies now aimed directly toward independence. The outcome of the Revolution assured by 1782 and the old colony character of North Carolina left behind, the new state was stirred by two contradictory impulses. One of these was nationhood as defined by her own territory. The other was participation in a nationhood common to thirteen units which, in collaboration, had won independence from Britain. In the end the second impulse prevailed, though not without difficulty.

But it was in the first impulse (state nationalism, based on its own boundaries, and sometimes called "particularism") that lay the stirrings toward state patronage of education. Whether these stirrings were predicated upon a contrast with what a number of the other states had done as colonies, or were now doing as newborn political entities, or whether they were the reflex of the democratic ideology now bursting upon the world, or in some degree compounded of both, it is difficult to say. Whatever the cause, the makers of the State's first constitution in 1776 wrote into that document (Section 41) "That a School or Schools shall be established by the Legislature for the convenient Instruction of Youth, with such Salaries to the Masters paid by the Public, as may enable them to instruct at low Prices; and all useful Learning shall be duly encouraged and promoted in one or more Universities."

In the English language usage of that period, capitalization of a word indicated emphasis. Hence it is not difficult to read from this section what the constitution-makers held important. "School or Schools," "Instruction of Youth," "Salaries," "Masters," "Public," "Prices," "Learning," "Universities," all are on a formal parity in the clause. Where chief emphasis would ultimately rest was yet in the womb of time. Nor has one hundred and sixty-five years of subsequent educational history in the State wholly clarified the "Public" mind as to the relative importances of all these elements of public interests. Nor was this possible in this beginning period. They are bound up together and only the interplay of political, social, and economic forces, some within and some without the State, would determine results.

A university, at least in name, was to be the first fruits of the impulse thus expressed in the Constitution. The State Assembly in 1789 chartered a degree-conferring university and set up a co-optating board of forty trustees to bring it into being and to nurture it. The Act fairly shirked direct financial responsibility of the State for the life of the institution. Escheated property and arrears in debts due the State back of January 1, 1783 were the resources voted—the first ultimately to prove of some real value; the second virtually equivalent to an unlimited moratorium. But the Act also held out the hat to the public, selecting two special incentives to induce gifts to the unborn institution. One of these was the privilege to a ten pound donor of appointing one scholar who would receive free tuition. Another was the naming of halls and colleges, up to six, for the most liberal donors.

Society, in this as in other ages, appropriately recognized the parity of money contributions with intellectual and spiritual ones in the building of the social state. Indeed, without a material base it is more than difficult to bring the other two to bear. Mohammed, until he married a rich widow, made scant headway in furthering the inspiration he had received from Allah.

While only three of the early buildings at Chapel Hill attained their names by this first and direct invitation of the State to benefactors, they were the first of a generous series that bear the names of men who gave in money alongside those who gave direct in brains and spirit. Indeed the number is not few whose gifts were compounded of all three forms.

The earliest Board of Trustees, named in the Chartering Act, working in a superheated political atmosphere, effected the beginning of a first building at the chosen site, Chapel Hill, in 1793. By January, 1795, with one teacher (elected as presiding professor), the University of North Carolina was declared open and a first student appeared in the month following. David Ker, the Professor, and Hinton James, the student, had the elbow-room of pioneers. James, before his student days were over, produced a paper on the title "The Pleasures of College Life." Since only the title, and not the text, is preserved, posterity has no clue to whether the emphasis was upon the period before or after the writer was joined by other students. Forty-one pupils and an additional instructor, Charles Wilson Harris, were recruited by the date of the first Commencement in July, 1795. A museum was begun, with an ostrich egg and a porcupine skin among the dozen or so of contributed specimens.

The members of the first board of trustees, named in the Chartering Act of 1789, were chosen from the groups of the business and professional men who in the main had led the State through the Revolutionary period and who, by 1789, had generally become converted to the desirability of uniting with the other states in a firmer form of union. The bulk of these could have been labeled as federalist in politics. Anti-federalism was particularly strong in North Carolina until well past the end of the eighteenth century. This factor unquestionably affected the chances of the State's essay in education as represented by a state university. To anti-federalists this represented a tendency to nurture federalist control, and federalism was becoming identified in the popular mind with class control. Business men, traders, large landowners, and professional men (mainly lawyers) saw the future welfare of the State bound up with political union with the other states. The new philosophy of democracy, breaking forth in France in violent political expression, was to superimpose itself upon an already strongly developing pioneer democracy in America. Hence it came about that those elements in America that were proponents of strengthening state powers, or enlarging state's functions, were invariably identified with old regimists. America, which had no aristocracy either North or South, almost convinced itself that it did. Business men, successful traders, and lawyers, all elements of the thrusting and restless middle class in Europe, in America were charged with "aristocratical" principles because their interest was seen to lie in strengthening governments—first a stronger union and, second, firmer state governments. And not a few of these elements in America had visions of becoming aristocrats in a new society, all oblivious of the rising tide of liberalism in Europe and the first notes of the knell of old regime privilege. And in pioneer America itself liberalism was far too strong to concede deference to anything beside material strength. So, with the single exception of the temporary rise and existence of a semi-aristocracy based on a sectional labor system of slavery, America has evolved no privileged class. But in the formative years of the republic there were real fears that there was danger of an imported system, a system that was already on an unsuccessful defensive in Europe. These matters, much hidden under other covering influences, were only partially observed in the era of the early history of the Union and of the American States; but they nevertheless profoundly influenced most of our social, economic, and political institutions, and their interplay one upon another.

The embryo University of North Carolina is a definite example. Launched out of the impulse of true liberalism, nevertheless the elements that had founded it came to be the political conservatives of its early period of life. This carried over into its middle period, when slavery and sectional interests still made conservatives out of those who still bore responsibility for the life of the institution. In all these years the political security of their control was nil, and hence it is not to be wondered at that the child they had produced remained a creature of chance. Whether and how it would grow, depended largely upon the shifting winds of politics.

Presiding Professors Ker, Harris, and Gillaspie had, each in his turn, proved too politically liberal by the end of the century to find firm trustee support. Yet the small student body seemed to have drunk from the same stream to the point of bladder inflation. Disorders of a violent sort characterized the embryo institution, to the great alarm of the conservative trustees, and led after the first six years to entrusting its local administration to a young

Princetonian whose political and social sentiments were in accord with those of the founders. This was Joseph Caldwell, a young Presbyterian minister only twenty-three years old. He became presiding professor in the midst of the semi-chaos at the University in 1799, largely because he possessed the confidence of William R. Davie, who was governor of the State in 1799, and whose influence upon the founding and launching of the University clearly entitles him to the distinction of being its father. Davie was a strong federalist in politics and, in North Carolina, ranked as a decided conservative. Caldwell, as a protégé of Davie and something of a prig in his earlier years, had a capacity for growth and adjustment that enabled him to weather the transition of the State's control from federalist to republican at the turn of the century. He continued in the confidence of the co-optative and conservative board of trustees and was made president in 1804. After this date came the period in which he gradually acquired the confidence of the now dominant republican element in control of the State. But this control was not definitely wrested from the old conservative (federalist) element before about 1812, and particularly in reference to the Board of Trustees of the young school at Chapel Hill. Amendment to the Charter in 1804 to provide for filling of vacancies in the board of trustees by the State legislature had been one of the first fruits of the rising strength of the Republican party in the State, but even so the conservative element yielded ground slowly. The partisan quality of Caldwell's outlook made his position as president uncomfortable enough by 1812 to cause his resignation, though he still retained the post of mathematics teacher. Robert Hett Chapman, another licensed Presbyterian minister, succeeded to 1816, when the Era of Good Feeling had so softened party asperities in the nation generally that it percolated even to the legislature of North Carolina and the now dominantly Republican board of trustees of its University. The fortunes of the school, without State support and now with little State interest, were at a low ebb; the staff and student members were about what they had been in the first five years of the University's life. Chapman was restless and seemed inadequate. Therefore Caldwell, who had at least stuck by, was called back to the presidency. It seemed to make little difference anyway, and this action would resolve the puzzlement of the Board.

Caldwell's second effort at administration (1816-35) seemed to make some difference for nearly a decade, using patronage as the yardstick of measurement. The student body increased to something over one hundred for the first time (1817-18) in the institution's existence and reached one hundred and seventy-three in the peak year, 1823-24. Thereafter there was a gradual recession to below one hundred in 1830-31, and again a slight rise to 101, the year that Caldwell died in office (January 27, 1835). But the variability of the student body in the State's institution at Chapel Hill before the Civil War period, any more than since the reopening in 1875, cannot be accounted for alone by the quality of its president. Other changing factors, economic, social, and political, were more potent as influences.

By the 1830's party lines had again become firm in State politics and the Whig party, spiritual heirs of the old Federalist party, were in the saddle. This party laid emphasis on national unity and an American system in national economics. It sought to depress the rising tide of sectional divergence predicated upon differences between North and South in social and economic matters. It controlled the State for thirty years except for a short period in the 1850's.

This party, in 1835, made David Lowrie Swain president of the State University in succession to Caldwell. Swain had been Whig governor of the State since 1832, for three successive annual terms —the limit allowed by the State Constitution up to the reform of that document in 1835. His party, now securely in power, made him president without much regard for his scholastic qualifications, and mainly to provide him with a berth as reward for effective party service. Nevertheless he was a practical man and administered the affairs of the institution with acumen and success. The student body increased from 89 in the first year of his administration to over 450 at the opening of the Civil War in 1861. This growth in the twenty-five years, while in part attributable to Swain and his political skill in creating confidence, plus his energy in certain internal improvements and increase of facilities, was in other part due to slowly increasing population and some increase of wealth in a wholly rural state.

Nevertheless, Swain's practical ability and his tie-in with the political party dominant in the most of this period did not extend to the possible goal of bringing the State government to adoption of financial responsibility for the life of its University. Of State appropriations there were none, nor any pressure toward this method of maintenance. The principle was accepted and fixed that the University must live "on its own." This had now been done through three quarters of a century. "Its own" was a fortuitous and quite irregular income, still derived from escheats, certain doubtful claims to Tennessee lands, gifts from the philanthropically inclined, and an occasionally authorized state lottery. All these sources were in steady decline, the possible exception being "gifts." Student fees, with the steady rise of patronage, had become the main resource, and Swain, up to the dread years of the Civil War, kept a balanced budget and even developed a surplus. Expenses were kept down by timidity in expansion. A faculty no larger than ten, and these with a generally low salary scale, seemed to Swain an appropriate method of husbanding the fortunes of the institution over whose fortunes he presided. Scholastic standards were low and kept so as if in appeal for greater numbers. Equipment and increased facilities made some advance, but not in proportion to increase in number of students. This increase in numbers was Swain's special pride, not only by reason of the financial security it wrought, but as furnishing proof that he was increasingly allaying the suspicions of the opposition party. The State's Rights party, called Democrats from the thirties on, contained a majority of the slave-owning and planter class. Swain, though frankly a Whig, had walked circumspectly and had emphasized the point that the State University was for the sons of all parties. Swain's nonpartisan bearing, plus economic and social forces now rising, took something off the edge of the party spirit, which had always reflected itself in effect upon the University. Hence, by the opening of the Civil War, had a census been taken, it would probably have disclosed a student body nearly in balance as to party background. Probably the two societies at the University, the Phi and the Di, were at that time the only remaining visible evidence of old party division between East and West, a geography which had ever tended to mark a difference in economic, social, and political outlook of the State.

That the spirit of the management of the University was Whig, from its head down through its faculty, its Board of Trustees, the legislature, and the State administration for so long a period before the Civil War had two primary important results. The first was internal. The student body never became a hotbed of sectional feeling and expression as the tide of national disunion arose. It would be an untrue picture to paint the University as filled with young cavaliers ready to mount and ride away to a clash at arms. Nor did the mere spirit of the management wholly account for this, though contributing importantly thereto. A factor of equal importance was the unadvanced standards of instruction in the University. Boys came there without preparation, the State as yet having no system of secondary education and not until the forties moving toward a popular demand for a public school system. Hence the young men in the University were as little prepared as high school boys usually are to absorb or reflect the currents of political forces moving on the face of the waters. Some sudden cataclysm or upheaval, demanding the application of youth's physical strength, was the only condition upon which spiritual maturity could be wrought. This was not untrue at a much later date of the University student body. Though there had been in the next half century a deepening and widening of the University's life, a tremendous advance in the quality of preparation of students, the quality of teaching and enlightenment at the University, the student body as a group in 1914-17 were little prepared to participate in or make contributions to the currents of thought involved in the clash of forces of the First World War. Not until the magic word "draft" was thrown out on the air did the students sit up and take notice. Then, with an avalanche of force, they turned away from sophomoric concerns to an interest in what it was all about.

So, in 1861, with the president and faculty imbued with the spirit of the moderate non-sectional party and with the students' unawareness of the electricity in the rising cloud, the bursting of the storm produced the other primary result, namely, a total collapse of the University in 1868-71.

This result was the product of external causes and their interplay upon the internal situation. When the volunteer tide and the first year of the Confederate draft law, 1862, had reduced student numbers to less than seventy, Swain sought to interpose with the Confederate government for exemption of the "seed corn." In this he was ultimately unsuccessful. But he thereby had injured his credit, and that of the University, with the war party. Old memories were awakened of Swain's party affiliations. He and his faculty were now held to have no heart for the cause.

Events were flowing swiftly and the collapse of the Confederacy in 1865, with the last of the fighting taking place right under the nose of the University, thrust Swain forward as participant in peace-making. Here his role was difficult. The terms of the victor had to be met. But whoever met them, or seemed to endorse them, would likely be a victim of public distrust. Bitterness of the defeated party was bound to be deep.

The comparative mildness of presidential reconstruction Swain endorsed, and from it gathered confidence that the old moderate spirit of the Whig party would be resurrected and get control of the State and its institutional life. This may have happened had not presidential reconstruction been discarded by the nation for the harsher policy of Congress.

In the meantime, while this point was as yet undetermined, Swain had more and more incurred the distrust and dislike of the defeated element. His spirited daughter Eleanor, as early as June, 1865, had married General Smith B. Atkins, who commanded the Federal troops occupying Chapel Hill. Here was proof positive to Confederates bitter in defeat that Swain and the University had never been sound. This marriage was made a *cause célèbre*, and a University complex was developed in the State. To denounce Swain and the University was proof of loyalty to the lost Southern cause. To defend him and seek a reinvigoration of the institution was the cue of old moderate men, mainly Whigs. These were now willing to accept the verdict of the war and make the best of the conditions of the peace imposed by the executive plan of Southern reconstruction. Between December 15, 1865, and July 1, 1868, a State government was in being in both executive and legislative branches that reflected this policy. During all this while Swain was under terrific fire from the old recalcitrants (Democrats), as if he were responsible for Confederate defeat. Yet he struggled hard, even achieved the unprecedented for the University. He secured a legislative appropriation of $7000 in 1866. In 1867 he secured the transfer to the University of the State's share of the Federal Land Scrip Fund. Thus a way seemed to have been found to save the University. And patronage began to rise in 1866, despite the superheated political atmosphere, the prostration of the State, and the discrediting onslaught upon Swain. He refused to resign and hoped for vindication in a calmer day.

2

THE UNIVERSITY UNDER RECONSTRUCTION; MRS. SPENCER AND THE REOPENING

ALL PROSPECTS for a compromised sectional peace were brought to naught in 1868 by the victory of Congress' plan of Southern reconstruction. This involved total submission to the will of the victor. A politico-military regime came in based on the will of Congress as declared in the Reconstruction Acts of 1867. Its immediate repercussion upon North Carolina was the founding of a Republican party to carry out the will of Congress. This party's constituent elements were carpetbaggers, scalawags, and the newly enfranchised Negroes. It took control under military auspices and proceeded to reorganize the institutional life of the State.

Under a new constitution, surprisingly respectable on paper, this violent, incompetent, and corrupt regime soon discredited itself. Meanwhile it seized the University, reconstructed the Board of Trustees, making that body, by its method of selection, dependent upon the will of the Reconstruction governor, W. W. Holden. This body ejected President Swain and the old faculty on July 24, 1868, and proceeded to set up a small partisan faculty of its own under the presidency of Solomon Pool. A month after this action President Swain died, the result of an injury from a runaway horse presented to him by General W. T. Sherman.

No financial resources were provided for the Republican University by the Republican State government, despite the orgy of bond issues and their corrupt expenditure that now disgraced North Carolina. These latter matters, plus Governor Holden's military violence, in reaction to the Ku Klux Klan, brought swift nemesis upon the Governor by way of impeachment in 1870. During the political turmoil the University died of inanition. It had no patronage, despite various schemes advanced, like free tuition, to induce attendance. Ridicule and scorn were two of the

15

weapons, harshly used, that finished the moribund effort. In 1871 its doors were completely closed by action of its own trustees, though they could scarcely be held to have been open since 1868.

The legislature that had successfully impeached Holden in 1870 was the product of a successful combination of old Whig sentiment and Democratic fervor, aided by the work of the Ku Klux Klan. Still the executive administration in the State remained Republican until the end of 1876, bolstered by the congressional reconstruction policy for the South. By this date old Whigism had lost its identity in the Democratic party in North Carolina, the party that was long to nurse the wounds of a crippled and arrested land. In 1876 it achieved control of all the branches of the State government. Simultaneously the Federal government removed its hand from the throat of the South and the long uphill pull began.

In the meantime a movement for the resurrection of the State University was gathering momentum. Indeed, this movement was coterminous with its closing.

The soul of the movement was embodied in a woman, a very remarkable woman, one whose quality—if ever adequately portrayed—must place her in the category of the nation's best. Mrs. Cornelia Phillips Spencer was the daughter of James Phillips, a young English emigrant from Cornwall who came to New York in 1818. The son of an Anglican rector of Evangelical views, young Phillips, twenty-six years old at the date of his arrival in America, had scholarly ambitions. Already he was well self-taught in the classics and in mathematics. In collaboration with a brother he set up in Harlem a private school for boys. He married a wife of Dutch descent in 1821 and came, by choice of President Joseph Caldwell, in 1826 to teach mathematics in the University of North Carolina. His daughter Cornelia had been born in Harlem the year before. He served the University as one of its stalwarts till his death in 1876, amid the gathering gloom of its near extinction.

The daughter grew up during the Swain regime. Her strong intellectual interests, her absorption of classical and modern literature, her poise and her tastes made of her a light that would have shone anywhere. Yet she lived out the bulk of her years in the little, restricted environment that was then Chapel Hill. Her passion was the University with which she grew up, and over its fortunes she was destined to suffer and struggle as few others did. Even now, if the place has a soul, its earlier embodiment was in Mrs. Spencer. In the twilight of the old University she supported and counseled Swain in his fight for survival. When the dark was complete she lit a candle and polished her weapons.

She was a thoroughgoing Whig in political thought, and the conquest of the South by force of arms, with the destruction it wrought in the Southern way of life, still left her poised on all issues other than the fate of the University. Here she turned, like a tigress at bay, and fought and fought with tooth and nail. By pen and speech and through her wide contacts with public men she led the assault upon the Republican force until it was dead. She was in at its burial, with scorn on her lips. Already she was laying the groundwork for a sane revival. Old Whigs were her hope, because she was practical. The roots of the University had been planted and grown in conservative soil. For this it had paid the penalty in the radical storms of the sixties. But spirit lives on, though often changing in outward form. It was this spirit Mrs. Spencer would re-evoke. She knew that as a party the Whigs' day was done. All its old leaders, Graham and Vance, Hale, and Moore, and many others had been forced along by political exigencies and finally absorbed into the post-bellum Democratic ranks. But there they were leaders still. Their leavening of the post-Reconstruction Democratic party was a fortunate circumstance for the history of the State for the next quarter century. It was a moderating influence, tending to dull the edge of Democratic party bitterness. It restrained somewhat sectional and race state action while yet there was danger of provoking national intervention.

Particularly was it fortunate for the chance of reopening the University, as Mrs. Spencer and her friends foresaw. Thus Democrats could be led to forget their old animosity toward Swain and the old regime and be induced to throw in with the now advanced plan of a State University free from political or sectarian bias. The plan was wise and adroit, but in no degree insincere.

For Mrs. Spencer, a keen diagnostician of institutional history, particularly the institution so near to her heart, dreaded the hampering and dangerous effects of either a partisan or a sectarian flavor upon a renewed University. The old University, for most of its history, had been manned in its faculty by a decided preponderance of Presbyterians, and its three presidents, 1804 to 1868, had been of this faith. This had been one effective cause of making it suspect, particularly by Methodists and Baptists, both now well-emerged as the largest religious groups in a state over-supplied with sectarian organizations.

By 1873 the friends of the University, almost entirely old Whigs, but not acting as such, procured an amendment to the Constitution of 1868 that abrogated the Republican device of executive control of University trustees. Circumstances were favoring, since at this date Tod R. Caldwell was governor in succession to the impeached Holden. Caldwell, now Republican, was orginally an old Whig, an old University graduate. Besides, he had read law under Swain. Thus as governor in 1873 he was not inimical to some plan for restoring the old state institution. Even so he balked at what he held to be irregularities in the method of the amendment of 1873. However, by 1875, the validity of the amendment was settled by a Supreme Court decision.

Meanwhile, acting on the assumption of validity, the State legislature had set up a new Board of Trustees in 1874, elected by joint ballot of the two houses. These were sixty-four in number, the active and effective element among them being largely old Whigs. Ex-Governors W. A. Graham and Charles Manly, Paul C. Cameron, B. F. Moore, W. L. Saunders, D. M. Carter, Seaton Gales, Walter Steele, Rufus Patterson, Judge W. H. Battle, and his son Kemp P. Battle made up a spearhead that practically assured results. Most of these men kept in touch with Mrs. Spencer at Chapel Hill, either by letter or by personal visits, heartening her in the campaign she was waging in the public press.

At its organization meeting, February, 1874, the board elected Graham permanent chairman and K. P. Battle, Secretary-Treasurer. A committee, headed by Steele, was set up to visit Chapel Hill. It was to make later report on the physical plant and the financial status of the defunct institution. This report was presented at a meeting in April. Chief obstacle to the purpose of the trustees was of course financial. Unless order could be restored as to assets and debts, and a resource found, then a new life for the institution would be doomed. Outcome finally was a sale of a portion of University property partially to satisfy importunate creditors. Debts thus scaled down, the next step of the trustees was to memorialize the legislature to restore the Land Scrip Fund that the Republican regime had invested in "special tax" bonds which a Democratic legislature had later repudiated.

The problem now was to induce the State to revalidate the Fund as part of a contract between the State and the nation and restore it to the University as an asset upon which the State would pay interest. This endowment was to be upon the original condition upon which the Land Scrip had been allotted, namely, that the State provide education in agriculture and the mechanic arts. The legal status of the new Board of Trustees having just been favorably settled by Supreme Court decision, it proceeded to promote a legislative bill for the restoration of the Fund. It set up a lobby, of which ex-Governors Graham and Vance were the most influential in the public mind, but of which D. M. Carter and K. P. Battle bore the chief burden.

This bill became the tensest issue in the legislature of 1875. It ultimately passed the lower house by only one vote. In the Senate it had easier sledding. This hurdle taken, the news was immediately transmitted to Mrs. Spencer at Chapel Hill. There, promptly gathering about her a few friends to share her keen pleasure, she disregarded the long-time absence of the old bell rope and climbed to the belfry of South Building to ring out the news to a dead village and the echoing hills around.

Restoration of the Land Scrip Fund meant the State's agreement to pay annually to the University the sum of $7,500 as interest upon the Fund upon the condition that it provide agricultural and mechanical instruction.

With this slender resource the trustees forged ahead. They commissioned the secretary-treasurer, K. P. Battle, to seek additional resources by way of donations from friends of restoration. Battle threw energy and skill into the task. Soon he had raised $20,000, perhaps a pitiable sum in the eyes of the present generation, but a prodigious amount to be raised by gifts from a people so completely bankrupt as were North Carolinians in 1875. Mrs. Spencer, in addition, inspired and led a movement that resulted in gifts for a beginning in necessary equipment.

Confidence mounted. The trustees met in May and adopted a plan of reorganization and set a date for opening in September. There were to be six colleges (we would now say departments). Agriculture and mechanic arts were given precedence. This was clearly out of deference to the source of the Fund that made re-opening possible. Then came natural science, literature, mathematics, and philosophy, presumably in order of proposed emphasis and importance. The curriculum was the product of a committee of trustees headed by Battle, the secretary-treasurer, who was proving a near genius.

Tuition was fixed at sixty dollars per annum, and room rent at ten, the latter low cost doubtless due to the disrepair and delapidation of the campus plant. In less rugged times than young North Carolinians knew in 1875, premiums would have been required to install and hold tenants. Students, however, and unmarried teachers were required to live in the dormitories, the latter apparently for the moral effect rather than for policing. The rules of the old University, which had been overstrict and often bred rowdyism, were passed to the discard by new bylaws. The principle of the new order was to put students on honor. Where this failed the president was to act. A future students' council was visualized to strengthen and encourage correct deportment. The active portion of the Board of Trustees, meeting frequently during the year 1875, on June 16 adopted a series of bylaws and elected six professors and an adjunct over against the opening in September. The professors were to head the schools (departments) created. The adjunct was to assist in the school of literature. Their names, in order of their choice and precedence, were: John Kimberly, agriculture; R. H. Graves, engineering and mechanic arts; J. De B. Hooper, literature; Charles Phillips, mathematics; A. W. Mangum, philosophy; and A. F. Redd, natural science. G. T. Winston was the adjunct in literature. Dr. Charles Phillips was made chairman of the faculty pending the subsequent election of a president.

Three of these men, Phillips, Hooper, and Kimberly, had been of the old staff under Swain, though only one of them, Phillips, had a connection at the time of the debacle in 1868. Both Hooper and Phillips had considerable prestige as scholars and teachers. Graves and Winston, youngest members of the group, had good scholarly preparation and some experience. Both were aggressive and forward-looking. Mangum and Redd were ocular proof that the trustees intended to avoid the charge of religious discrimination—a charge often hurled at the old University in the long years of Caldwell and Swain. Under both, Presbyterian influence had generally been held to dominate the institution. In the new faculty Mangum was a widely influential minister of the Methodist Church. Redd came fresh from the editorship of the Baptist paper, the *Biblical Recorder*.

Sectarian suspicion nevertheless was long to survive, particularly on the part of Methodists and Baptists. Its later manifestations, however, were based on other issues than exclusion from the teaching at Chapel Hill. For Battle from the first was astute enough to be well aware of the danger from that source. An Episcopalian himself, he was liberal enough in subsequent recruitment totally to disregard religious affiliation. It was politic to do so, but Battle made it honest practice on its merits, practice that all his successors observed until it became fixed tradition. Meanwhile the social order grew up to the point of indifference to the creed of a teacher.

In the postwar University, politics was the enamel that glazed the mind of the faculty. The spring of its renewed life was Whig, but the Whigs that renewed it were now perforce Democrats. The Democratic party was now dominant and long to remain so. It remained parochial and nursed the wounds of the South. Its immediate enemy, the Republican party, nursed the Negro and sought control. Therefore the University, child of the State, could not long have existed had it not conformed in general coloration to the dominant political creed. Failure to do so had been its doom in 1868.

In its new era it failed to breed men of extremes. Battle himself, the carry-over of three of the old faculty into the new family of seven, and the preponderance of old Whigs in the active element of the trustees, insured moderation. Yet there was uniformity of political views, and uniformity, though tinged with moderation, is not an atmosphere that quickens movement in a democratic society. Not to labor this point, it still must be noted that up to the turn of the century there was not to be found in the faculty a member who openly advertised other than Democratic party principles. There were doubtless a few Republicans on national issues—for by this time the faculty was being expanded —and with little regard to sectional origins. But such members found themselves in an atmosphere that could easily grow frigid to political unconformity in state issues. This uniformity, leavened with a large lump of discretion, was not a matter of consciousness or purpose. Rather was it an unconscious sharing in the state-wide view that order in the State, social and political, was yet bound up with the dominance of the Democratic party.

Yet it was in these years of discretion and uniformity that the habit was fixed, and it hardened into tradition, that members of the University staff should refrain from active participation in matters political. This tradition, at long last, is now being undermined. It had its useful day. Nevertheless it entailed certain positive disservice. Men of the University faculty, some of whom, then as now, were well qualified by capacity and intellectual training to make useful contributions to the science of government were definitely isolated. Also it fostered in the minds of laymen the false notion, yet widely prevalent, that college teachers are peculiarly unfit, by intellectual slant, to participate actively in practical affairs. One outstanding result of this notion is that professional teachers are shunted out as a class, yielding the field to "practical men," mainly lawyers, who run the government in all its branches. Hence the professional teacher, in part by his own delinquency, yields up to others the advantage of a name—the label, "practical men"—just as all working America yields the name "Labor" to the minority of workers who labor with their hands, in mine and factory. Only this group is supposed to sweat. Thus it gains advantage of the moral implication that it carries the rest of the world on its shoulders.

3

THE SELECTION OF A PRESIDENT: KEMP PLUMMER BATTLE

THE ELECTION of a president of the University was deferred in 1875, after W. A. Graham had declined the burden by reason of failing health. Graham was perhaps the best trusted man in the State, despite all the political exigencies and party fermentations since 1860. A lifelong Whig in political principles he had had a distinguished public career until the South's defeat in the sectional struggle.[1] This choice would have been an admirable one from most standpoints. Graham had the confidence of the Democratic party, now on the eve of gaining control in the State. At the same time he commanded the respect of the Republicans. Living at Hillsboro, near by the University, he preserved an intimate interest in its affairs. An alumnus of Caldwell's time, he was a trustee from 1834 to 1868, and again in the reorganized board of 1874 until his death in 1875. In close collaboration with Mrs. Spencer, the Battles, and others mostly of Whig lineage, he was the acknowledged leader among public men who labored to bring the University back into being.

Just after Graham's death, August 11, 1875, reopening ceremonies took place at Chapel Hill in September. With no president as yet, the trustees had named Dr. Charles Phillips as chair-

---

1. As speaker of the State commons from 1834 to 1841 he was elected to the U. S. Senate in 1840. Whig governor of the State from 1845 to 1849 he became secretary of the Navy under President Fillmore in 1850. He was candidate for vice-president on the ticket with General Winfield Scott in 1852. Strongly opposed to secession, he led the opposition that defeated the movement in the first North Carolina convention. In the second he yielded when Lincoln called for troops from the State. Even so he sought to go out by the door of frank rebellion rather than secession. Secession prevailing, he became a senator in the Confederate Congress. When secession was extinct he gave his energies to reconstruction along sane lines. Supporting Johnson's plan of reconstruction he was elected to the U. S. Senate in 1866. The rising tide of congressional reconstruction blocked his seating, along with other Southern senators-elect.

man of the small faculty of seven. During the first academic year —September to the following June—about seventy students were enrolled. This was a beginning, though a modest one. It was in the midst of the direst poverty, in the midst of the tensest clash of political forces in the State. The clash was to make an end of "reconstruction" from without and make a beginning of self-reconstruction, a heavy task—political, social, and economic. For those who had found the energy in the midst of poverty, discord, and confusion to lend a hand to restoring the University, the event of its reopening in 1875 was a heartening thing. To them a new vista was opened, down which they believed the State would build a wide highway, perhaps planted to trees, great trees which would cast their generous shade on successive generations passing that way.

Through the first year of operation of the reopened University the question of a president was fermenting in the minds of that narrow segment of public opinion that gave any thought to the institution. The trustees held it steadily in mind. Two views developed. One held for some Southern leader of note in the Confederate cause. Another, "that the financial and other difficulties required a native of the State, known to and acquainted with her people, peculiarly identified with the University and loving it with his whole soul, a Democrat, yet not an active politician, and therefore not offensive to men of the opposite party. He must also be a man of experience in dealing with men and not easily ruffled into loss of temper or vindictive retaliation by opposition however malignant. Above all he must be a one-ideal man, and that ideal the University."[2] The first view was the product of uncooled sectional fervor, plus the conviction that an illustrious Southern name would give immediate prestige and bring large patronage.[3] It was the view of that segment of public

---

2. This statement is Dr. Battle's own definition of the view that prevailed in the decision of the trustees when he was chosen. (Kemp P. Battle, *History of the University of North Carolina*, II, 115). It is a characteristic bit of the unaffected simplicity that marked the man, mirroring the image he held of himself. Curiously, it was a picture much nearer the truth in most details than most men could paint of themselves.

3. The outstanding illustration of which this was already true was General Lee's headship of the college at Lexington, Virginia.

and trustee opinion that was strictly sectional and Democratic in antecedents. It was strengthened by younger men influenced by the sectional conflict. The other view, the one that prevailed, had its roots in old Whig soil. Though Whigs for the most part were now Democrats their spirit survived. And, for immediately practical purposes, it was a majority in the trustees and complete in the executive committee.

Therefore upon the day of election, June 17, 1876, Battle was chosen by a three-fifths majority of the twenty-five trustees present and voting.[4] For the rest of a long life he completely immersed himself in the life of the institution which he loved so well, proving the thesis that he was a "one-ideal" man. He had no enemies and was determined to make none. He would make friends, rather, by proving friendly. By this time the Democratic veneer on his Whig soul was sufficiently thick to eliminate questions of his party orthodoxy. Also the University and the State were yet so close to Republican rough handling that he held it wise to give no occasion for injury, political or otherwise, even from "the opposite party." That party might be in the saddle again! And yet Battle's idea was not entirely precautionary. He honestly held, without ever formulating his view in exact terms, that the State's University ought not to be subject to the wavering fortunes of party. All parties would do well to serve it inasmuch as its role was to serve the State irrespective of party. Here he was right and wise. He builded better than he knew, even though he could not then foresee the all-but-unbroken Democratic party control for the following three quarters of a century.[5] But for Battle the beginning of this wisdom was memory of the tragedy of 1868 when the University of Swain, of the Whigs and Presby-

4. General Joseph E. Johnston received five votes. General Matt W. Ransom one, and Montfort McGehee three. McGehee, a large landowner of Person County, had been state secretary of Agriculture. His candidacy was apparently launched on the ground of the University's commitment to agricultural education by the reception of the Land Scrip Fund. Jefferson Davis had been promoted in the Democratic press, but his name was not introduced at the election.

5. Unbroken except for the fortuitous supremacy, 1897-1901, of the Republican-Populist combination, the result of an agrarian movement.

terians, was caught up in the swirl of political currents and was drowned.

Now resuscitation had taken place, allowed by the Democrats who were now taking over State control from Reconstruction Republicans. This allowance, fundamentally, was an act of grace to the Whigs the party had absorbed. As a party measure it was done without enthusiasm. It had granted the Land Scrip Fund by the narrowest margin possible. Beyond this the University was again to live on its own. But Battle had faith that this could be done. Had not Swain, in prewar times, made a prosperous institution? This had been accomplished out of tuition fees of a steadily increasing student body. Battle believed this story could be repeated. While this was being demonstrated he would bother the State little, in the meantime thankful for its tolerance. It was a timid idea but eminently practical, and for two very potent reasons. One: the State was utterly poor, financially dead-broke. Nor had it ever had the idea of a university supported directly by State appropriations. Two: the reopening had not been a spontaneous action of the Democratic party. Thus the State, in all but continuous control of this party from then till now, waited on two things before it ever took the institution to its bosom. These were the gradual, very gradual economic advance and a corresponding gradual development of confidence in the institution's worth. The "opposition party," destined to remain but an opposition in State politics, came also to have confidence, disarmed by the Battle policy of general appeasement. Sons of Republicans soon felt as much at home in Chapel Hill as any other citizens, though uniformly taught by tactful Democrats throughout Battle's period and for some time after.

Hence Battle fitted the need as the glove fits the hand. He would offend nobody, individual or party. In many ways he was spiritual heir to President Swain, but with a clear eye for some of Swain's mistakes. He adopted some of Swain's methods outright. He would know the boys personally and make them a nexus to the parents' confidence. Sound financial management of the shoestring income was his especial care. He was never concerned much about curriculum standards. These were to advance in time, but from other pressures and at the hands of other men.

Dr. Battle was sprung from a Revolutionary ancestor, Elisha Battle, who as a young man had crossed from Virginia into the Tar River section of North Carolina about 1744. The first two or three generations of Elisha's descendants had remained primarily interested in land and planting, while taking a due part in local and colonial (afterward state) affairs. Subsequent generations, while retaining an interest in land, became townsmen and lawyers, mainly in Nash and Edgecombe counties, and showed a capability for business and finance. It was a prolific family and produced a number of able representatives in each generation after Elisha Battle. Originally, the family were strict Calvinists in religious affiliation, adhering to the Primitive Baptist Church and influential in its councils. With transition to the towns, to business, and the law, the family in its main branches became Episcopalian and has remained so to the present time. There was an appreciation of education as a way of advancement from the first generation on down till now. Two members of the family were students at the University in 1800.

In reaction to the social, economic, and political conditions in eastern North Carolina during the early and middle periods of our national history, the Battle family developed traditions and practices characteristic of a successful combination of the tenets and outlook on life of a lesser gentry and an upper middle class. Bearing, manners, and tastes were sound. Enterprise in business and the professions, particularly in the law, combined with a strong addiction to integrity as an essential of success, characterized each successive generation. Success in business or the legal profession was not used as an avenue to political preferment. Political employment in minor offices was sometimes accepted, but as a result of popular demand, rather than political ambition or personal intrigue. Lawyers in this family, of which there have been many, have generally been the type that embodied the safest guardianship of the funds and estates of widows and orphans. In business as in law the family's representatives have generally illustrated an integrity that tended to become a tradition.

Kemp Plummer Battle, of the fifth generation from Elisha, was the third of six sons of William Horn Battle. William Horn Battle was a lawyer. He became a Superior Court judge and was advanced to the Supreme Court Bench (1852-1868). During the same period he was professor of law at the State University (1845-1868 and again from the reopening in 1875 to his death in 1879). Being Whig in politics Judge Battle was in a favorable position to aid and influence the State's readjustment to national relations so long as moderate counsels had a chance of success. But with the application of congressional reconstruction in 1868, Battle and men of his stamp were thrown out of the picture. He retired to the practice of law with two of his sons in Raleigh, Kemp Plummer and Richard Horn, Jr. When the University was reopened, he came back to Chapel Hill and reopened the Law School under the presidency of his son Kemp Plummer.

President Battle was born in 1831. At twelve years of age he came to live at Chapel Hill.[6] He entered the University as a stripling and was awarded a degree in 1849. He then became a tutor in Latin and carried through to a Master's degree in 1854. Meanwhile, he crowded in the study of law. He moved to Raleigh for its practice, following an ante-bellum custom of attorneys to ride out "on circuit" with the Superior Court judges. Battle's trend was toward corporation and business law. He had no strong penchant for political affairs, such as was usually active among young and aspiring lawyers. Nevertheless he was gradually drawn into the strong current of political forces that were moving in the decade of the fifties. He aligned himself with the conservative forces and backed such Whig leaders as George E. Badger, Willie P. Mangum, and ex-Governor Graham in their efforts to stem the course of the South toward disintegration of the Union. He was in the May Convention of 1861, which took the State out of the Union and, along with the other Whigs, yielded with regret to the course of events that had made the action inevitable.

During the war Battle still ranked as a conservative, though this role was increasingly difficult to sustain. In the period of

---

6. Judge William H. Battle first moved from Raleigh in 1843 to educate his sons in the University and himself to teach law.

presidential reconstruction[7] he became state treasurer by election in 1866, but lost this office in 1868 when congressional reconstruction swept the State clean of all the old order. He had also been a trustee of the University since 1862, an interested and helpful one, but he lost this post when the State Reconstruction government set up by Congress took the institution over in 1868.

Battle never flirted with political office after this dread year. But his experience with men and measures in the rough and tumultuous period of the sixties, besides producing political nausea, had well-qualified him to accomplish a task of superlative social importance, the restoration of the University.

The reopening of the University almost simultaneously with the removal of the hand of the Federal government from the control of the State's political machinery seemed a propitious time, with a promise for its future. The event had been slowly in preparation for several years, with Battle among the prime movers. Tied in as he was by family and tradition and by personal attachment to the prewar institution, he believed that here was a work he could successfully accomplish. Besides, he saw little promise for himself in the broken political and economic order and had small taste for the conditions of warfare in those fields. He would leave those fields to others, sanguine in the faith that firebrands and disunionists had now been disciplined and presumably would now behave. The era to follow would presumably be shaped by reasonable men, men who accepted in completely good faith the decisions of war. Events were to prove that the prospect was not nearly so simple. Resentment and resistance were long to survive, particularly against the helotage of the South in national economic and political affairs, a helotage bulwarked by the victor party through the use of the Negroes as voters.

Mrs. Spencer was pleased but surprised at Battle's willing acceptance of the presidency, not that she underrated the importance of the post, but rather that she misread his tastes and his out-

---

7. Battle was among the first to seek pardon of President Johnson under the Amnesty Proclamation of May 24, 1865. His petition, dated June 13, 1865, casts light on both his action and his views. The original copy is in the State Archives, Historical Commission, Raleigh.

look upon the political future. Evidently had she herself been a man she would have been out fighting where the pikes were thickest.

Despite Battle's precocious, energetic, and successful career as a student at the University in the late forties and early fifties he was never a profound scholar, then or afterward. His reading was diligent, though not coherent. He gathered facts like moss, but he never organized them into an effective pattern or placed them in due relationship. He had some flair for business management and business law and had had some practical experience in these fields.[8] In appearance Dr. Battle was of medium height, with a figure that was quite erect until extreme old age. Then he stooped a bit both in the shoulders and the knees, but he never grew pudgy or rotund. He walked much for pleasure and in a deliberate and observing way. He carried a cane, often using it for pointing, for jumping a ditch, or mounting a stone. He was conservative in his dress and liked a "cape" for his shoulders long after this garment had been discarded for the overcoat. He wore a rounded beard and preferred his upper face shaved. He had an excellent brow and blue-grey eyes. His manners were uniformly frank and affable and were touched a bit with mid-century courtliness, especially toward women. His conversation was spritely, and the spirit behind it was lively and animated. His will to humor and wit was stronger than the results obtained. He was fond of robust stories, but weakened many of his own by hearty laughter before the point was reached. The type of his wit was in the fashion of his times but it never bore a sting to embarrass a friend. Always cheerful, affable, and optimistic, he reflected those virtues in all his contacts, with students, colleagues, and acquaintances. Looking backward, it is difficult to imagine any other available man better fitted to take up the task Dr. Battle assumed in 1876. This task involved weathering a period of great poverty in the State, a period of popular uninterest in education and, particularly, a fear of costs. It involved disarming unfair and carping criticism of the beginning made, making friends

---

8. He had represented some of the few industrial corporations in the State struggling for survival during the sixties and had become president of a small railroad company in the same period.

for the institution, and removing it from the dangerous shoals of politics. These things were largely accomplished in his time but not completed in his administration. Others carried on along the path he had blazed out, ever widening it until it assumed the proportions of a broad highway.

Dr. Battle's imprint upon curricula and standards of instruction was less important than his other work. Besides his own modest attainments in definite scholarship, these were conditioned by the poverty of the institution and the lack of preparation of would-be students. The dearth of resources narrowly limited equipment and facilities. It forbade appropriate expansion of the teaching staff until increase in student numbers had made this a little possible. Even so, from the first there were a few able men, well-grounded in their subject matter and willing to sacrifice adequate remuneration in the interest of ideals. Slow increase[9] in student numbers had several causes. The mood of the poverty-racked State was generally callous toward systematic education. The marriage of the ideas of democracy and public enlightenment was not yet effected. The concept that education was a luxury was widely held, and few could afford luxuries. This mood changed very slowly before the last decade of the century. There had been some lip-service and some largely futile gestures during Reconstruction times, these made by the Republican control as a bid for confidence. It therefore remained for the grueling years after 1876 to see a slow dawn of interest in a public school system. Before the Civil War, certain weak foundations had been laid and some advance made on the work of a structure. But war and the ensuing political storm had wrecked all these. Plans must now be virtually new. Though the public was generally apathetic, a few idealists persisted, and a weak state system gradually arose.[10] In the last quarter of the century this system conduced little to

---

9. In 1876, Battle's first year, 112 students matriculated. In 1891, the year of his retirement from the presidency, the number was 248. Thereafter, improving economic and social conditions produced a more rapid rise. At Battle's death in 1919 the student body was near 1,800.

10. This system, at the mandate of the State, was locally financed and locally controlled, as seemingly befitting the theory of democracy. It dragged and lagged in some localities and made some healthy advance in others, thus reflecting varied and spotty local economic and social health.

the benefit of the State University, though in that period the latter's standards for entrance were scarcely beyond the quality of an adequate high school of later times. In the meantime the University in Battle's period of administration had little grist to grind from the public school system, the public high schools not yet having come into effective being.

The best-prepared boys that came to the University in this period were those who had passed through the mill of some of the surviving privately owned and privately conducted "Schools," "Academies" or "Institutes," of which there had been quite a crop in ante-bellum North Carolina. Practically all of these private schools, numbers of which were organized on a military plan, succumbed during the war. Afterward some of those which had been the most successful reorganized and reopened.[11] The best of the limited numbers of students turned out by these schools tended to pass on to the University, where curriculum and standards as yet scarcely strained their energies. These, the ambitious ones, set a good pace for their less well equipped college contemporaries and culled such honors as they chose. The prompting influences that drew them to the University were several in kind. Perhaps the most important was prestige. The name "University" was the first element in this prestige. It was the State's top and only institution of supposed higher learning, however undernourished and uncultivated by government. It had age almost equal to that of the State itself. In its prewar life it had been the stomping-ground for the liveliest, the best socially fit, and the most ambitious of the youth of the State. There unconsciously, particularly under Swain, they had got a feel of

11. Oak Ridge began a new and continuous life in 1875 under J. Allen Holt. Horner's School reopened at Oxford under J. Hunter Horner, and Bingham's School at Mebane under members of the family whose progenitor had founded it in the early part of the century. These schools, together with others that did not survive the war, rendered valuable service to many youths of the State. In them boys of vigor and spirit learned much of the value of discipline and teamwork, and many achieved a sound grounding in mathematics and the classics—the two fields of study held most in emphasis in the prewar period. Those that survived, that is to say resumed, in the postwar period were those whose founders, or their family successors, had a combination of practical ability in business management and sound educational ideals.

political citizenship, and interest in public leaders, in political trends in State and nation.[12] Most of the political leaders of North Carolina, and many who went out to other sections of the nation, had passed through the University, receiving such training and influence as it gave. This training, without set purpose to do so, laid largest emphasis upon public life and political matters, or else was itself a reflex of these. Hence the names of leaders who had passed through the University, however embryonic as a "University" it may have been, were a drawing force for students after the Civil War as had been true before. "Fashion" still worked in the interest of the institution, though fashion and poverty were hard to combine. The students who, against odds, found their way to its doors remained sectional in viewpoint to the end of the century, but hardly as violently so as many became when they passed out into public life, where they were confronted by the public problems of the South's readjustment to a reintegrated nation. Their speeches and essays in their literary societies, or on public platform at Commencement occasions, were likely to bear sectional captions, and the body of such thought and feeling as they contained long turned on sectional rights or flung out in resentment at sectional wrongs. Southern leaders, men of political and military careers, were habitually acclaimed as peerless.

12. This statement would probably hold for most colleges in the South in ante-bellum times, perhaps also for the North. At the University of North Carolina political coloration was at first Federalist and afterward Whig.

4
THE ADMINISTRATION OF KEMP PLUMMER BATTLE

THE REGIME OF DR. BATTLE was a period of germination. Seeds were planted and began to sprout. Later some of the strongest bore ripe grain for the State. The Law School was reopened in 1877 under Dr. Battle's father, Judge W. H. Battle, a man who, by virtue of experience at the bar and on the bench, and as a productive scholar in publication in the field of law, was well equipped to give the school prestige. His age, seventy-five, at the date of reopening, was the chief threat to continuity of the school. Yet when he died two years later (1879) his son, President Battle, rather than see the Law School lapse, assumed the active duties himself and continued as its one-man teacher of law until Judge John Manning was brought in in 1881. Under Judge Battle the school was given something of the modern pattern—existing for the sole purpose of teaching. It thus varied in important details from the ante-bellum practice of a well known and well established lawyer taking into his office a young man or two desirous of becoming members of the profession. There they "read law" in a sort of apprentice relation to their instructor. At the same time they gained valuable experience as his assistant in drawing briefs and doing other tasks set by him. Likewise there was opportunity to attend him in the courts and gain direct knowledge of the tricks of the trade. Many of the best known and most successful ante-bellum members of the bar and bench came up through this system. The embryonic Law School at Chapel Hill had the advantage of sanction by the trustees and a place in the catalogue as offering instruction in the law. Otherwise, especially for some years, its relation to the University was somewhat attenuated, being mainly personal and by implication. There was, of course, no admission of financial responsibility by the State. Its life was dependent upon its own income. It could easily have died with the passing of the elder Battle had not the son, President Battle, taken upon himself the personal burden, in addition to his regular teaching and administrative duties.[1]

A pioneering effort of Battle's University which was of large future consequence was the founding of a summer normal school. Its purpose was primarily to train teachers for the greatly undernourished and inadequate common school system. The concept was appealing, the need was great, and the execution was particularly successful—as long as the State government made it possible to continue. Battle and his friends, effective men among the trustees, had procured from the legislature a grant of two thousand dollars annually for the project and had launched the normal school in 1877. It ran seven successive summers (to 1884) and comprised a total enrollment of around 2,500 teachers within the period. It gave a decided boost to the weak teaching profession in the State and served as a model for imitation in numbers of Southern states. By-products of the main effort—to better equip teachers—were quite important. A sort of *esprit de corps* was created. Perspective was gained on the needs of the profession. At the summer session of 1878 the teachers organized the "North Carolina Teachers Association" and furthered a movement to effect county associations throughout the State. Committees were set up to make a study and report on the State school system and to propose remedies for its weaknesses. The State press strongly endorsed the Normal School idea and its progressive achievements. The successive governors, Brogden, Vance, and Jarvis, officially and personally stressed the high need of greater State effort to educate its people and threw their weight behind a continued appropriation. A normal school for Negroes had been opened at Fayetteville at the same time. Dr. Battle in Chapel Hill took high pride in the movement and its reflex influences on the life of the University. Unfortunately for the latter, the legislature in 1885, while continuing the same appropriation, thought it wise to bring its benefits more immediately within regional ac-

---

1. At this time President Battle was also professor of political economy, constitutional and international law, actively giving instruction in these subjects and sometimes others additional.

cessibility to the teachers. Hence it took the unwise course of dividing the fund into four parts ($500 each) for normal schools to be provided at four regional centers (Asheville was to be the extreme western one, and Elizabeth City the eastern). It was the very worst sort of educational statesmanship, the dispersal soon affecting the death of them all—as should have easily been foreseen. But the plan and the precedent of a summer school for teachers at the University had been set and was destined to be revived later, with notable success.

The beginnings of a medical department (later school) was made by the University in 1879. A physician, Dr. Thomas W. Harris, an ante-bellum honor student (Class of 1859), trained for his profession in New York and Paris, had set up a practice in Chapel Hill and soon made an arrangement with the trustees to conduct a medical school. Harris became dean, and two other professors, one in chemistry and another in botany and physiology, were to give courses. The financial arrangement was without responsibility of the University, as was its control. It was a weak effort from the first, but continued until 1885, when it folded up with Dr. Harris' resignation after practical acknowledgement of failure and some local discredit growing out of suspicion of grave-robbing for purposes of specimens. This six years' existence of a medical school had also laid a precedent and suggested a continuing need that the University later returned to and made a more sustained and successful effort to fill. It also illustrates the process by which the University has grown into various fields by absorbing private enterprises set up around it. A later example was a successful school of pharmacy; and a more recent one, the Institute of Government, a pioneering enterprise of Professor Albert Coates of the Law School.

Battle's friendliness and affability, overlaying the recognized sincerity of his purpose to build the fortunes of the University, began early to bear certain material fruit. His mind had never been disimbued from the idea that private gifts were one of the most practical ways to secure the development of the University. Donations were sought and gratefully accepted, a "Form of Bequest" being annually printed in the University catalogue. Thus, in the third year of his administration, the Deems Fund was founded to aid needy students by loans. This fund, by addition, had increased to considerable importance by the end of the century, has been soundly administered through all its history, and is still, at a figure around $200,000, a most useful agency in the hands of the institution. Steady adherence to the purpose of its founder contradicts the history of many other eleemosynary foundations the country over. While this and numerous other gifts to the University, most of them for special purposes, have proved greatly useful to the institution, they could never become sufficiently great in sum total to meet ever growing needs of further development. This was necessarily true in the very nature of the case.

As wealth increased in the country at large in the next half century, as great fortunes arose that pyramided themselves in the hands of men so capable and skilled in exploiting economic opportunity, the impulse arose to make munificent gifts for the general good. Educational institutions were founded, or old ones strengthened, on a scale in America that has never been duplicated at any other time in any other country—though the process is old in the history of civilization. But even at its peak in America generous donors were largely estopped in the case of state institutions. The fundamental cause lay in two obstacles. One, the would-be benefactor could not expect to shape and mold a state-controlled institution to his own especial views as to how it could best serve. Two, few felt that their fortunes, however large, should supersede the obligations of the State to care for its own. Hence state universities largely missed the flow of wealth at its tide, though there was undoubtedly an indirect influence in awakening state governments to their own obligations. Yet it is uniformly true that it takes great skill to give considerable funds to a state university without at the same time convincing the state that the need has been supplied. The acquisition of a building, to perpetuate the name of a donor, was not so difficult to effect. It was once in considerable vogue and added most usefully to the University plant. Mr. Carnegie's munificence was so large and so widely scattered in America and Europe that it marked a great epoch in library expansion. The University of North Carolina attained its Carnegie Library, the first appropriately organized armored bastion of this fundamental need it had ever possessed.

Here again, with the wave of growth and expanding needs following the First World War, the Carnegie Library passed into a new structure provided by the State, now itself grown economically strong and more intellectually advanced. As for Mr. Carnegie, one can take satisfaction in the thought that he knew that he had once opened the portals of heaven and poured out the rain on the parched fields. Nor did the University miss its adequate share when the nation-wide disease of "stadiumitis" gripped the country. The volcanic upthrust of the athletic impulse in American institutions threw hot lava over the whole social scene. The public caught fire. The national preoccupation with wealth-getting now had a rival in matters athletic. There was much to commend it. *Mens sana in corpore sano* with qualifications. Faults there were in this invigorating flood. The trend toward "professionalism," and the vicarious participation of the ninety-nine per cent on the side-lines vitiated the evolution. Still the ninety-nine per cent were out of doors, they were diverted, given their thrills. In the colleges and universities danger lay in overemphasis on this one interest and possible forgetfulness of the main purpose of their existence. Stadiums piled up. Alumni loyalty and the competitive impulse assured that state institutions, particularly the capstones, had their share. Private donors were not hard to find. The athletic wave promised a long sweep in history. Moreover a thing carved out of the hills and built of stone seemed a thing enduring.

Even so, here too was another illustration that the march is onward. First gifts may sometimes be badly located, may prove inadequate for the swelling tide. Obliteration or reconstructions may become inevitable. In such case decent intervals will be observed so that the shade of the donor may have time to readjust and take consolation in the thought that he served his day and once was greatly acclaimed. It only proves the inevitable and the necessary. Society is dynamic and will advance. Stadiums, bell-towers, and such like material monuments are well in their kind and enable the University to "keep up with the Joneses," that progressive family so well distributed in America. Nor have strictly cultural benefactions been a small stream. Warm-hearted alumni with cultural ideals now and again break through the inhibition to supplement state provision of the University's needs. Hill Music Hall is the latest instance.

These things have come in the years since Battle's time, in the years of expanding economic and social life of the nation, in which North Carolina came gradually to share. They came after the State had finally taken its University to its bosom, though the heart in the bosom has beaten with something of irregular vigor. The nuances of public mood, of political and economic exigencies, have effected results. Even so, results are potently rich in quality, the University so outstanding among all its contemporaries of the Southland that Battle could but gasp to behold it.

President Battle, eternally industrious, found the extra energy in 1880 to revive an alumni association. This was just in time to supply a definite need. A crisis was approaching in finance. Student fees and the Land Scrip Fund made up a resource far short of pressing need. The Land Scrip Fund was fixed and stationary, at $7,500. The student body had grown only slowly and was now around 200. The income from fees was reduced by the State requirement of free tuition to one student from each county, and free tuition to clergymen's sons and prospective clergymen. In addition, fee income was further reduced by the liberal policy of accepting students' notes in lieu of cash fees. Hence actual income in 1880 was about $14,500. The faculty stood at ten heads of departments, two subordinate instructors, a librarian, and a bursar. The Law and Medical schools were yet on an autonomous basis, not on the University budget. The trustees cut faculty salaries ten per cent. President Battle took the field in an effort to raise gifts from private sources. This failed, the weak spring having now run dry. Then a true course was struck in an urgent appeal to the legislature. This course was taken with diffidence and hesitation. Battle feared it would be an admission of defeat and failure. Moreover, the agrarian tide was rising that was shaping toward a separate agricultural and mechanical college. This would mean the loss by the University of its nest-egg, the $7,500 from the Land Scrip. Further, an appeal to the legislature for money out of taxation would bring the University squarely up against clerical opposition, a formidable threat to the very existence of the institution. The proposal of an appeal for State funds was hardly known to the public before the heads of three sectarian colleges—Wake Forest, Trinity, and Davidson—immediately joined in a memorial to the legislature against the grant of any tax funds. Certain outstanding laymen of each of the three churches, Baptists, Methodists, and Presbyterians, signed the memorial with their respective college heads.

The Battle appeal, to make it more palatable to the legislature, contained a proposal to double the county students that were to receive free tuition and room rent. To the memorialists this feature particularly seemed a shrewd device to gather students for the University and to diminish their own. They argued that present admission of one county student free was not honestly applied, that rich men's sons secured the appointments rather than the aspiring poor. Behind such arguments, compounded of jealousy and the competitive spirit, was the more fundamental conviction that education beyond the common schools should be shaped under clerical influence. This conviction much later was brought clearly into the open by J. C. Kilgo, head of the Methodist's Trinity College soon after its removal to Durham. Kilgo's lines had been brushed out for him by two predecessors, Braxton Craven and John F. Crowell, the first having long guided the Methodist effort at college building at the old Trinity in Randolph County, the second having become the head of Trinity upon its removal to Durham. Kilgo, succeeding Crowell in 1894, infused new life into the fight of the denominational colleges against State aid to its University. In this fight he found a doughty young co-fighter among the Baptists in the person of Josiah W. Bailey, recently come to the editorship of the *Biblical Recorder,* the influential Baptist church paper formerly edited by his father. Bailey had taken the place of Columbus Durham, the notable Baptist spokesman against State aid in the previous decade. Bailey gave a trenchancy to his paper that greatly increased its influence, and was politically shrewd and aggressive. Kilgo was a bold and formidable fighter, armed with a strong conviction and the spirit of a zealot. He sought to submerge the issue as one of competition. He phrased it boldly as "Christian Education" *versus* "Godless Education." Through a newspaper he founded in 1896, the *Christian Educator,* and the clerical militia in his own church, he carried the fight home to all the towns and rural communities in the State. During the years of the heat of the strife, the hapless University student, particularly of Methodist or Baptist origin, was made to feel that he was a sort of pariah, that he had separated himself from God's people. Particularly was this true in strictly rural communities, where church control was more nearly a social fact.

The Presbyterians cooled first in their opposition to the State's support of its University out of taxation. Several causes would seem to account for this (1) The old long dominance of this church at the University in the years of Caldwell and Swain. This had established a tradition, a tradition of alliance and favor between the two. (2) Davidson was in the southwestern area of the State and drew its patronage from that area and upper South Carolina. These two areas were fairly compact socially and Presbyterianism was strong in both. (3) There are those who would contend that Presbyterianism, transplanted to America, first warped from Calvinistic dogmatism in essential feeling and grew more progressively liberal in a free atmosphere. By the late nineteenth century this may have been a fact that bore some part in diminishing self-consciousness on the part of this sect. It was ready to live and let live in the matter of all those social agencies designed for social welfare.

Meanwhile the initiation of the long-drawn-out conflict between the University and the sectarian colleges was in the appeal of President Battle and the trustees for a State appropriation in 1881. The movement had been carefully prepared during the year before. An alumni association meeting in June, 1880, had laid the foundations. When the legislature met in January following, another meeting of alumni was held in the State Capitol under the very nose of the lawmakers and in their session rooms. A banquet was tendered by the alumni to legislators and their friends. The session's officials and influential members were intrigued into responding to toasts. The trustees had been primed and had published and spread widely a well-argued and disarming body of resolutions showing the University's needs, its service, and its proposed services. Battle and his ablest lieutenant in the faculty, G. T. Winston, were ready with a brief for the University in elaborate detail, to be spread before the legislators at work. These two settled down as lobbyists at the session. Newspapers plunged into the issue of the proposed subsidy. It had a good press, though the *Biblical Recorder* stoutly led the cohorts that backed the memorial of objections the sectarian colleges had launched. Outcome was a victory for State aid by an annual appropriation of $5,000.[2]

Importance lay in the principle established and in the frank admission by the State of its obligation and purpose to support the University. The sum was small but the State's resources were small. Yet to the University it was a lifeline cast just in time to save the ship from foundering. The $5,000 was to continue annually for four years. Meanwhile the denominational forces girded their loins for further combat. The University was discreet in its victory, strove to build internally, and emphasized the healthy religious and moral tone prevailing at the University. Battle was not insincere in this claim and made continuous effort to have it true. Episcopal and liberal in religious thought, nevertheless a few generations back he was Calvinist and still could understand and gauge the force of rigid religionists. He must not exult in this beginning victory. Four years would soon be up. The policy of annual appropriations must be made permanent. There would be continuing opposition. But time and new currents were running in his favor. The governor, Jarvis, in 1885 was again strong in the University's support and in his message to the legislature recommended a total of $37,000, of which $22,500 was for operation and the remainder to clear up certain debts. The church colleges and the leaders of the denominations, Baptists, Methodists, and Presbyterians, made a strong organized fight when the legislature met but were successful only to the extent of reducing the final over-all appropriation to $27,500. Also they had blocked the proposal in the bill to increase the number of county students to receive free tuition.[3] In the end this part of their victory served the

2. The University request had been for $7,500, coupled with a proposal to increase the number of county students with free tuition from one to two. It was this feature, assuring more students at the University, that the rival denominational colleges most feared.

3. See for this whole controversy of the denominational schools with the University over State support of the latter a very excellent work of

interests of the University well in respect to its finances. It was now in much better position to expand, to increase its faculty and other facilities looking to the end of higher standards, and this was an immediate result. The faculty ran up from nine to fifteen. There had been several hundred candidates for places in this increase of six.[4] Trustees winnowed them down to a much smaller number and made their choice of four full professors and two assistant professors, among whom two lived long in the service of the University, Professor Thomas Hume and Professor W. D. Toy, both of Virginia, and added qualities to this staff that have set precedents. Although Dr. Battle disclaims any influence of religious affiliation in the choice of the additions,[5] it is a curious fact that two were Baptists (Hume and Toy), two Presbyterians, one Methodist, and one Congregationalist. Yet this circumstance, sop to the sectarians, seems not to have diminished the charge that the University was under Episcopal influence, the one church that had no competing college in the State and whose general number of communicants was very small in the whole population. The increased appropriation of 1885 had also a direct reflex in curricular changes and enlargements, not overlooking increased instruction in moral philosophy, or branches relating to agriculture and the mechanic arts.

In the financial adjustments in the legislature in 1885 over University affairs, the University, as already mentioned, lost the appropriation of $2,000 for the summer normal school which had been conducted on its campus since 1877, and which Dr. Battle held justly to have been one of its greatest successes. Not until 1895 was held again a summer school at the University under new arrangements that brought to life again the old values that Battle had ascribed to the sessions between 1877-84. Thus there were losses as well as gains in 1885, with the foreshadowing of a second loss in the rising contention of the agrarian leaders, especially L. L. Polk, for a separate agricultural college. Though

---

Luther L. Gobbel, *Church-State Relationships in Education in North Carolina since 1776*. Duke University Press, 1938.
    4. Battle, *History of the University of North Carolina*, II (1868-1912), 333.
    5. *Ibid.*, p. 335.

there was still danger to the University from sectarian sources after 1885, the principle of State aid had virtually been fixed by that date. The danger thereafter would probably reflect itself in the meagerness of support as church organizations influenced legislative temper.

However, another issue was rapidly gaining importance of large significance to the University. This was the rise of an agrarian movement, largely shaped and directed by L. L. Polk. An ex-Confederate veteran of Whig antecedents and views, Polk had opposed secession but went into the ranks as a private, rose in rank to major, and had an effective military career before the war ended. Upon re-entry into civil life as a practical farmer, he became a fiery exponent of agricultural reform in the new era of the South's necessary economic readjustments. Of Irish stock, he was purposeful and pertinacious, a strong advocate of the causes he made his own. Already a successful farmer and merchant, he established a weekly newspaper, *The Ansonian,* soon after the war, and urged attention to agricultural interests. This paper was the progenitor of his later paper, *The Progressive Farmer,* established in 1886, which since that date has had a continuous life and usefulness to agricultural interests. Meanwhile Polk was the effective mover behind the State's creation of an agricultural department and became the first commisoner (1877) of the department. As early as 1872 he had advocated, while the University was prostrate and closed, the establishment by the State of an agricultural college. His ideal was an institution devoted solely to the teaching of practical agriculture as a means of bringing the State into agricultural prosperity, of which her soil and her climate gave great opportunity. He had organized farmers' clubs throughout the State and brought them into harmony in the State grange movement.

Polk had not been hostile in 1875 to the reopening of the University, though he had held that the Land Grant Fund should have been devoted to a separate agricultural college. He watched the experiment of the use of the Fund by the University and came to the conclusion that a successful combination of agricultural and liberal arts education was a practical failure for the interest he had most at heart. He thereupon increased his efforts for a separate college, this of course involving the loss by the University of the Land Grant Fund. Matters came to a head in 1887. Through county clubs, mass-meetings, and the organization of a state-wide Farmers Association for political pressure, immediate results were attained in the legislative establishment of the Agricultural and Mechanical College at Raleigh.

Meanwhile Battle's position as head of the University, and possessor of the $7,500 Land Grant Fund, was not an enviable one. The University had been re-established on this fund in 1875 and, plus gifts and meagre student fees, had lived by it until the first annual appropriation of $5,000 additional in 1881. This annual addition had been increased to $15,000 in 1885, and thus in this year its income from the State in sum total was $27,500. Battle had been thoroughly honest and energetic in his endeavor to organize and operate the University on lines he regarded as a sound interpretation of the meaning of the Federal Act of 1862, by which the Fund came to the University through the hands of the North Carolina State government. Specifically his interpretation boiled down to a liberal arts college giving prominent place to scientific education in subjects "relating to agricultural and mechanical arts." He could do no more with the funds at hand. To this theory of the University's obligation he consistently held during the whole period of the possession of the Fund.

The University's offerings and organization to meet this obligation were given first place in the University catalogue. During Battle's first year he visited the Connecticut Agricultural Experiment Station, and soon after influenced the North Carolina legislature to set up an agricultural experiment and fertilizer control station in connection with the University. An able head was chosen by him to conduct this department. Battle later visited Tufts College, Sheffield Scientific School at Yale, Massachusetts Institute of Technology, and numerous other institutions to inform himself on methods and achievements of schools of applied science. He added to the slender resources of the University in agricultural and technological literature. As a result of his gleanings of information, he set up a four-year course in applied science leading to the degree of Bachelor of Science. He swung over the State, addressing school commencements, agricultural fairs, and informal crowds at county court houses during intermissions of court. Upon invitation he delivered addresses upon agricultural subjects in neighboring states. All the while under criticism by the churches and the rising farmers' movement, he constantly insisted that the University was meeting its obligation, meeting it well, within the limit of the resources at command; that lands, herds, farm machinery, and technological equipment were not supplied by the State. And even if it were, Battle held, the best interests of citizens would be subserved by a liberal arts education first and foremost in equipping men's minds and releasing hidden forces. In his speeches and propaganda he especially emphasized the idea that a prospective farmer ought not to be educated for farming alone, that general culture was a prime need. This approach to the problem, he held, would raise agriculture, and those engaged in it, to the bracket of other professions, e.g. the law, the ministry, and medicine. He seems to have overlooked the fact that in his generation education for these example professions was not always, or very generally, grounded on a liberal arts education in advance. Still his diagnosis was not undiscerning in face of the fact that, with the collapse of the old slave labor system in the South, agriculture came to be looked down upon when labor upon the farms must be performed by white men if a sound agricultural system was ever to be attained. Battle's real point was that agricultural labor was as honorable as any other, but that classism was bound to result if the agriculturalist was educated only for the plow-handle and the milking-stool. His notion was to combine the two—education of the "head and the hand" at one and the same time, if agriculture was to be raised to the dignity it deserved.[6] This was the high peak he reached while making the effort to retain the Land Grant Fund.

Yet the forces were much against Battle in the setting in which he strove. In the whole Southland there was an impatience to come to immediate grips with the problem of an improved agriculture, a goal very much to be desired. This goal seemed to the many to be more swiftly within reach by divorcement of agri-

6. See Battle's anniversary oration, *The Head and the Hands, Problems of the Day*, delivered at South Carolina College, 1886, printed as a pamphlet by Messenger Publ. Co., Goldsboro, 1886.

cultural education from liberal arts colleges. Eventually this was the pattern that generally prevailed in the Southern states and most of the North and Northeast. In the South, past social and economic systems and the seeming necessity for radical reconstruction were the main explanation. In the North, a different agricultural tradition and the absence of state universities are suggested as the main factors.

When it became ultimately apparent that the fight with the churches and farmers' movement, whipped up from the top by Polk, was a combination too strong to resist, Battle, practical man that he was, yielded assent and agreement to the agrarian demand for separation. The legislation that effected the divorcement in 1887 subtracted the Land Grant Fund, leaving $20,000 to the University from the hand of the State. Thereafter its task was to conquer popular confidence in the broad area left it. And, beginning in Battle's time, the rising tide of the scientific spirit enabled it to edge in, in a notable way, upon the applied sciences other than agriculture. At the date of consolidation (1931) it had a school of applied Science second to none in the South and a school of engineering with its head erect among the best. It lost the school of engineering in the consolidation process of 1931-36, when the Agricultural and Engineering College at Raleigh, the Woman's College at Greensboro, and the University at Chapel Hill were brought together in one system under one head, under the title, The University of North Carolina. With the transfer of the engineering school to Raleigh, the School of Applied Science at Chapel Hill and the School of Liberal Arts were combined into one school under the name of the College of Arts and Sciences, in which the old School of Applied Science turned up in the reorganization as the Division of Natural Science and remains as one of the three great divisions of the University.

It is doubtful whether even a much greater educational statesman than Battle could have saved the unity of North Carolina's effort to further the uplift of her sons in matters social and economic at the time of the original division. The circumstances he, his faculty, and the trustees dealt with seem too overwhelming. Clerical influence and the church schools were on his back the whole time, questioning the right of the State to support higher education out of tax funds raised by levies upon sectarians who had their own colleges supported by the voluntary principle. Then the agrarian leaders, not wholly free from political motives and aspirations, had found a good whipping-post in the University, a college striving to do too much on far too little. "Practical farmer education for farmers" was a catchy phrase, implying a sure-fire method of agricultural regeneration. The future was to prove that regeneration was a process slow and long, that many factors bore on the problem other than courses in practical agriculture. Probably the presence in the South of so large a landless class made the development of a tenant system inevitable. This cuts squarely athwart a sound agricultural economy as visualized by Polk and the early post-bellum agrarians.

No pronouncement is intended upon the depth of the sowing of the Agricultural and Engineering College in its history of independence from the University. Advance in agriculture has certainly been made. Even farm tenancy is slowly declining in percentage to land operated by owners, and here lies hope that the gap between agricultural education and a sound agricultural system may ultimately be bridged. In technology the Agricultural and Engineering College, in its later period, has made solid contributions. These have been made in conjunction with the drift of technology and of capital from the North, and they are reflected in the present character of the State in matters economic.

The implication of failure implicit in the loss of the school was absorbed by Battle with a resiliency that characterized the man.[7] It was an episode. The University's life was fated. It would go on. In his concept of education the liberal arts had always been of predominant importance. The skies had now been cleared. The State had chosen to repose responsibility for agricultural education elsewhere. His institution would go on training well up to the point of fitness for making special choice of careers and work in a work-a-day world. The composite result, he believed, would be an intelligent citizenship going about the business of building the State's welfare, political, social, and economic.

For the remainder of Battle's administration until his retire-

---

7. See Kemp P. Battle's *History of the University of North Carolina*, II, 374-79, for his reactions to the fact of separation.

ment as president in 1891, there was a very slight decline in total student numbers. Explanation lay in the Act of 1887, which cut off free tuition to the counties for one student each. Yet the drop was not in proportion to the counties. The actual year of his retirement saw an access to numbers beyond any previous year since reopening in 1875. This increase thereafter was continuous and was largely the product of a combination of forces. Paramount among these was an upthrust of public interest in popular education. The State was beginning to awake to its need. Leaders appeared. Charles D. McIver and Edwin A. Alderman set the pace, forerunners and guides to a new emphasis upon education that profoundly affected the State within the next twenty years.

Battle had been president of the University fifteen years when he resigned of his own volition in February, 1891. Only sixty years of age, in sound health and mental vigor and possessing full confidence of his board of trustees and colleagues in the University, he chose to divest himself of the responsibilities of his office which he had borne with such patience and urbanity as to conquer the respect of all the elements in the State who wished the University well. Never jealous of anyone, and to the end an appeaser of opposition, he felt himself entitled to get out of the spotlight. Criticisms and opposition he had borne with great outward equanimity. Inwardly he had suffered, and in his modesty he was now confident that some other wise choice for his post would clinch and advance all that he had struggled for. It was a propitious time for his retirement. The conflict with the clerical forces was in temporary lull, and might not have to be resumed. The State had apparently fixed the principle of its obligation and purpose to sustain the institution out of public revenue. True, this sustenance was yet remarkably thin, but he believed it would increase in proportion to the proof the University offered that the investment was sound.

There had been some physical expansion by 1891, particularly the great Memorial Hall that was expected to furnish an adequate and enduring auditorium. Alumni funds had been a chief reliance, whipped up by the great human impulse to honor the dead. President Battle, the University, and the alumni were proud of the tediously acquired structure for some few years. In our passion for "firsts" there was the boast that it had no equal in the South. This was probably true, but on the wrong side of the ledger, both from a utilitarian and an architectural standpoint.[8] It stood on the campus for forty-four years (dedicated June 3, 1885; torn down in 1929), evoking the wonder of succeeding generations of students and visitors, a not uncommon experience of man, from the moundbuilders till now, when he looks upon what the ideas and tastes of his predecessors have wrought. Material planning of the University of North Carolina in its physical aspects could not but be long delayed in view of the poverty of the institution until after the turn of the century.

This building and certain other material projects, e.g. a gymnasium, had cost Battle severe effort to extract money from alumni and friends. Few things tended to clog his spirit more than continued solicitations for gifts from a clientele little prepared to give. He had once had assistance from certain friends in this always distasteful work, even certain dependable bagholders when friends ran short—as they always did under such a system. Mr. Paul C. Cameron was the ablest of these, was always generous of his time and effort and his own resources to aid the University. So were W. L. Saunders and Walter Leak Steele of their time and effort, though they were not men of wealth as was Cameron. These three men died in 1891, and the end of their long services to the University must have seemed to Battle the end of an era.

8. See Arthur P. Link's "History of the Buildings at the University of North Carolina," unpublished MS., Chapter 8. An Honors Thesis, 1941.

5

THE ADMINISTRATION OF GEORGE TAYLOE WINSTON

GEORGE TAYLOE WINSTON succeeded Battle in 1891 by unanimous vote of the Board of Trustees. His selection was in essence automatic and wholly natural. Winston as a young man, an honor graduate fresh out of Cornell, where he had instructed for a year, had come to the University of North Carolina as an adjunct professor in the year of the reopening in 1875. The following year, when Battle came in as president, Winston was raised to a full professorship in the classics. Thereafter, in the gradual enlargement of the faculty from seven to some twenty men of all ranks, none, by the time of Battle's retirement, had outdistanced Winston in effective service to the institution, either in its internal organization or in its external relations. There were a number of very able men in the group by this date, real specialists in their respective fields, some of whom were stalwarts of the University for long years to come: Francis Preston Venable in chemistry, Joseph A. Holmes in geology and mineralogy, Joshua W. Gore in natural philosophy, John Manning in law, Walter Dallam Toy in modern languages, Eben Alexander in Greek, William Cain in mathematics, Horace Williams in mental and moral science, R. H. Whitehead in medicine, Henry Van Peters Wilson in biology, and Carl P. Harrington in Latin. Battle, by choice, was relegated to the newly created chair of history and in this was destined to be happy and cooperative until his final retirement (1907) in the midst of Venable's administration, the third of his successors.

This faculty that Winston headed for five years after his succession was a real faculty by the very best standards of measurement. There were some eccentrics in it, a few whose eccentricities were to become accentuated through the years they served the University. This is not unusual, particularly in a professional group closely associated with each other, with succeeding generations of college students in a small village built around the traditions of a college then just one hundred years old. Some of the eccentrics were naturally so, the products of temperaments not unusual in any large or small group of individualistic intellectuals. Some had cultivated eccentricities, a coloration taken on deliberately as a means of attracting attention, again a thing not unusual in a university group. Of the first type Doctor Thomas Hume was a fine example. His departure from the normal came to disclose itself in the form of irritability, probably engendered by very weak health. Its outward manifestation was an impatient sensitivity to the conduct of boys and their lack of appreciation of the very fine things he had to offer from his rare scholarship in English prose and verse. Student conduct in the University was not always perfect in his day, not yet disciplined by a common standard of good taste that restrained the exuberant and the thoughtless. Dr. Hume, a natural gentleman, never comprehended that manners are a matter of growth, subject to the uneven influence of background and training. To him the precept "be a gentleman" was so easy of application that he was constantly astonished that it was not universal. Nor did he make allowances for the mischievousness and over-high spirits of juvenile minds now first away from the disciplines of parents and home environments. Thus his reactions to small but irritating antics of some of his students from year to year established a tradition that was handed down in successive college generations, much to the hurt of his very fine teaching and the ripeness of his scholarship. Yet the sober and serious students in his classes, those who had a passion for acquisition of broader horizons in English literature, he led into fair pastures. His passion for Shakespeare, his mastery of interpretation of this the greatest of all English literary geniuses, opened to many minds a storehouse of scholarly content upon which they have fed down through the years. Dr. Hume was slight in figure, his body bent as with too much learning and by the books he trundled in his arms across the campus from his home or the then small library in Smith Hall. Always was he affable and courtly in manner until provoked in classroom by either a dullard or a mischief maker. Then he poured out his scorn and vituperation, and in such beautiful and liquid prose that the chagrin of the disorderly student at the occasion was partly compensated for by Dr. Hume's technique. One can but regret that this man, with the love and mastery of his subject not exceeded by any of his successors in the University of North Carolina, could not have played out his career in a later stage of University manners—after the matter of discipline was no longer a problem.

Other men who stood out notably in the faculty of the nineties, some of whom fortunately survived to quite recent times, were Francis Preston Venable, Henry Van Peters Wilson, William Cain, and Eben Alexander. Venable, an assiduous worker in all the numerous tasks that fell to him in a small but growing University, was a scientist first and foremost and was already by his researches, with inadequate facilities, becoming widely known for his work in chemistry. He visualized the great future of his science and was one of those in this period who were plowing the soil for the great crop of chemical advances that characterize the present age. Venable was a man without poses or foibles. Intellectual honesty was the keynote of his character, both as a scientist and in his relations to the faculty and to the student body. Despite his immersion in his science he had practical wisdom and much administrative ability. In Alderman's administration, following that of Winston, Venable was a sort of balance wheel in the machinery of the institution guided by the less experienced Alderman. Thus he was natural successor to the latter.

Professor William Cain came into the faculty in 1889 to head mathematics and engineering. There had been no prohibition laid on the University in respect to instruction in the latter field when the Agricultural and Mechanical College was established by the State in 1889. Hence, despite possible duplication, courses grew up in the University that laid the foundations for an effective engineering school at a later date which came into competition with the State College[1] at Raleigh. At the period of recent con-

---

1. The school at Raleigh, receiving the Land Grant Fund when it was subtracted from the University was chartered under the name of the North Carolina College of Agriculture and the Mechanic Arts. It was popularly designated as the A. and M. Later (1917) the title was officially

solidation of the University at Chapel Hill, State College at Raleigh, and the Woman's College at Greensboro into one state system for higher education, the Engineering School at Chapel Hill, with the larger part of its faculty, was transferred to the State College at Raleigh. It was the early addition to the faculty at Chapel Hill of men of Cain's qualifications in engineering, so closely tied in with applied mathematics, that caused the growth in this direction, later cited as duplication of the State's efforts, and furnished much of the argument for consolidation and a reallocation of respective fields of activity, supposed to save the State much expense. Cain was a man of unusual endowments in both his fields, though the bulk of his published output was in the field of engineering. He had been a young soldier in the late stages of the Civil War, then had taught in the South Carolina Military Academy (now the Citadel) at Charleston, and came to the University of North Carolina in the fall of 1889.

Cain never married. He had rooms in a private home, his quarters resembling a crow's-nest of the things he liked to have about him—old pieces of furniture, for which he had a sentiment, books of his profession and general reading, scientific journals in mathematics and engineering, musical instruments, particularly violins upon which he performed for his friends. He was meticulously observant of his social obligations, preserving longer than any other man in the modern faculty the practice of calling at the homes of his colleagues and other friends at least twice a year as a matter of social duty. He loved lively conversation and was a good raconteur. He loved hunting quail and was proud of his skill with his gun and dog. He loved to fish with rod and reel and, in the summer season, would resort to the North Carolina highlands to enjoy this sport and to renew his spirit by a long summer vacation in the wild. This habit he retained to the end of his life, though growing deafness had lost him his music and his keen satisfaction in teaching and in social intercourse. Recognized by the faculty as one of its first lights, he had automatically been chosen by that body as one of the first Kenan pro-

---

changed to the Agricultural and Engineering College and, later still, in popular speech, the institution is referred to as State College.

fessors when the Kenan Foundation was first set up. The increased stipend meant little to Major Cain, for his wants were few and his tastes quite modest; but he took quiet satisfaction in the confidence and respect the action reflected. Of his own volition when his strength was sapped he sought retirement as emeritus professor and died in 1930.

Eben Alexander, by way of Yale and chairmanship of the faculty of the University of Tennessee, came to the University in 1886 as professor of Greek. Alexander was a representative of the spirit that the modern age has ascribed to the Golden Age of Helas, when the Greek race was at the peak of its culture. His inherited refinement and gentleness of spirit, acted on by his love for Greek literature of the classical age, had produced in him a quality of charm that set him apart in the faculty of his period. To the faculty and students alike he was unconsciously an influence toward poise, to a catholicity of view, to an appreciation of beauty in art and in life, to a rounded culture. A tattered seller of berries at his back door was to Alexander a subject of human interest little less than a man of his own intellectual stature. Even the student who pursued no classical studies felt his influence upon the campus, an influence making for light and healthful learning. His spirit long abode at Chapel Hill after his death in 1910.

Henry Van Peters Wilson, biologist, possessed the most incisive intellect in the group of able men whom Battle had assembled and in 1891 had passed on to Winston and his successors. Slight of frame, quick in movement and of a nervous temperament, Wilson embodied a passion for his own science plus a clear-sighted judgment of the role of science in an awakening age. He had no taste or inclination for administrative functions. Research, exploration, laboratory experimentation bounded his activities. Even so, as time went on, he developed a keen critical faculty of a constructive quality relative to university policy, curriculum, and coordination of effort. An incisive and pointed speaker in the faculty, few measures that were unsound or faulty ran the gauntlet of his analytical mind. He turned on the light as to where measures headed. Sharp wit combined with a pungent and caustic tongue, with little regard concerning whom he offended, served to keep others off his toes even though they might sharply differ with his premise and his conclusions.

Wilson had had excellent preliminary training for his work at Chapel Hill. Born in Baltimore in 1863, he had passed through the public school system of that city and then into Johns Hopkins University in 1883. Here he had come into the orbit of the scientific spirit just then being planted in American university circles in an organized way. Hopkins, founded in 1876, represented a new force in American higher education. Research, a new spirit of inquiry born in mid-nineteenth-century Germany, had been its basic purpose. A faculty of free and fresh minds had been gathered there whose will was to push on beyond old horizons. It became the first graduate school in America and the model for imitation by the whole field of American institutions. Never diverting to the policy of money-getting in the era when its imitators were lining their vests with great donations from captains of industry, it ultimately became overshadowed by these. Yet it had set in motion the whole process of modern scientific research and the constructive application of science among a pioneer people of untold energy.

Wilson was a clean-cut product of the Hopkins atmosphere in the years of its first burst of energy. He came to Chapel Hill in 1891 as professor of biology. After a decade of brilliant work his influence resulted in the differentiation of his field into three separate departments—biology, botany, and zoology. Of these he retained the headship of zoology for over thirty years following.[2] He gave to the renaissant University of North Carolina a most considerable proportion of its impetus for science and lived long enough to guide it into successful accomplishment. Wilson possessed a vivid and forceful personality, was intolerant of shows and pretense in others, never sought popularity among the students or faculty, and commanded deference by his sheer intellect and transparent honesty. After nearly fifty years of service, when he died in 1939, only his colleagues and the scientific world in his own and related fields knew that a great figure had gone. The

2. Robert Erwin Coker, in the *Year Book of the American Philosophical Society*, 1939, has made the best assessment of Dr. Wilson's scientific achievements, as well as an excellent projection of the varied preliminary stages of Wilson's preparation for life's work.

political and popular world mind of the State scarcely knew that he had ever existed.

George Tayloe Winston, who in 1891 took charge of a faculty of such men mainly assembled by Battle, was the most fortunate choice the trustees could have made, given the time, the circumstances, and the setting of the institution. Born of a forceful and pushful family in eastern Carolina, Winston had been trained at Annapolis and at Cornell. His mind was a powerhouse of energy, open to the new forces that were in the wind in the post-bellum period. He had been Battle's ablest lieutenant in the practical guidance of the institution since its reopening in 1875. He had practical sagacity and was adroit in avoidance of the pitfalls set by the clerical and lay opponents of the University. Strategy to Winston was of first importance, bold strategy that Battle would scarcely have dared use. Never by nature an appeaser himself, he nevertheless went along with Battle's policy, taking practical pains to make the policy work. When he came into the leadership himself he advertized no open change, but proceeded to fight with sharper weapons. The University was still numerically small, less than 200, and still not out of the woods in the confidence of the State and the danger from the churches. Increase in numbers was Winston's first care. He developed skill in advertizing, he curried the State and brought the institution, its faculty, and other advantages before the minds of the people. He was an adroit and forceful public speaker, ready in wit as in reasoning. He believed strongly in the recrudescence of the South but had few illusions as to the huge task ahead. The principle of leadership was all important, and this leadership must be evoked and prepared by sound education. Like Walter H. Page, his friend and in some degree his mentor, he leaned away, as far as it was safe, from nostalgic sentiment about the South's past and advocated preoccupation with the present. His inherited Whig convictions made him a nationalist, his training and comprehensive understanding made him see the national picture whole.

Winston's own practical energy was largely aided in results by virtue of a general new emphasis on popular education now arising in the State, to which he largely contributed. Recent University men, Alderman, McIver, Noble, Alexander Graham, and many another, were calling on the State to throw off its lethargy, to educate its sons. Practical means were employed. A teachers' association was revamped and re-energized. Winston became the president of the State teachers' assembly in 1889. His idea was to plant firmly in the popular mind the concept that the public school system, the multiplying high schools in the towns, and the University must be an integrated whole. Each to strengthen the other, leadership from the top, sturdy support from the bottom, would create a new North Carolina. Alderman and McIver, both burning with zeal for popular education, were unleashed as a team to work the miracle of a popular awakening. They accomplished large results by popular educational meetings throughout the counties of the State. They conducted teachers' institutes, widely infusing new energy and a new self-respect in the poorly prepared teacher profession.

Dr. Winston, mindful of the University and public school benefits which had accrued from the experience with a summer school at Chapel Hill for eight years (1877-84), a school that had been regionally dispersed in 1885 by legislative enactment, resulting in a large loss of momentum, determined upon a renewal of the plan at Chapel Hill. By 1895 he succeeded in the project, widening the plan to include students as well as public school teachers. Thereby the first could gain credits to advance their academic careers, and the public school teachers could advance their certification, renew their information, and increase their zest for their tasks. A singularly fortunate choice was made to direct the school. Edwin A. Alderman knew more of the teachers of the State than any other man. They knew him better and more favorably than any other one man in the profession. Thus Alderman, under Winston's practical backing, laid the foundations and erected the framework of a part of the University system that has endured as a permanent link between the University and the State public school system. Alderman was added to the faculty in 1894 as professor of the history and philosophy of education.

A summer Law School session, in collaboration with Dr. John Manning, was opened by 1894 and the Chief Justice of the State

Supreme Court, James E. Shepherd, was brought in to give it momentum and prestige. In the same year (1894) a summer school in geology was set up at King's Mountain, in the western part of the State, under a new and dynamic member of the faculty, Collier Cobb, who was to have a long and important career at the University. Contiguity to the supposed mineral sections of the State accounts for this instance of dispersion, but it was not without results to the Geology Department at the University. Cobb, as a one-man geology school at King's Mountain, made the western area geology-conscious, and added greatly to the University's repute in linking up with the practical needs of the State.

Dr. H. V. Wilson in this year launched a summer school in marine biology at Beaufort, N. C. Wilson's work here was to be continuous throughout his life. By 1900, in collaboration with Johns Hopkins University and the Universities of Virginia, Georgia, South Carolina, and North Carolina, the Federal government was brought to establish a nationally financed Fisheries Biological Station at Beaufort, whose continuous history was largely shaped by Dr. Wilson.

Internal reorganization of University departments and agencies was a particular interest of Winston as president. The library resources of the institution, formerly dispersed in various repositories on the campus, were assembled in one building in 1886, and effective library administration was set up with a small paid staff in 1893. Accounts of the University were systematized. A classicist in scholarship, Winston nevertheless possessed capacities not usually found in the pure scholar. Thus he was never productive as a scholar except as a teacher; but he more than made up for this in his skill at administration and management. When Battle handed over the reins to Winston in 1891 the State appropriation to its University for the biennium, 1890-92, was $22,500 per year.[3] Winston maneuvered the legislature up to $27,500 for 1892-93 and to $30,000 for 1893-94. At the same time income from tuition was rising by virtue of increase in numbers.[4] Yet Winston's

3. State Treasurer's Report, p. 13.
4. Numbers stood at 197 for the academic year 1890-91. At Winston's last year, 1895-96, the number was 534.

five years were restless years in the life of the State and full of uncertainties, political and economic. The agrarian distress had given rise to a Populist party, seeking to wrest control from the old-line Democrats, whom they regarded as static. The outcome was political fusion between Populists and Republicans, this combination securing control by 1896. Winston had ridden the rising storm, and it had been through the growing pressure of the Populists in the legislature that educational appropriations had been increased during his administration. However, when the combined Populists and Republicans were in power, the Republican wing largely had its way in state control and appropriations fell off again through their four-year period of rule.[5] Social tumult had accompanied the political overturn, ushering in the old question of the Negro's place.

In the meantime Winston was wrestling anew with the last onslaught of the sectarian groups upon the principle of State taxation for its University. New vigor had been infused into this old opposition by the arrival of John C. Kilgo as head of Trinity College, now removed to Durham and securing the financial patronage of men of wealth, especially the Dukes, economic entrepreneurs with genius for organization. Kilgo, with his trenchancy and vigor, secured early after arrival in the State a strong influence upon Methodism. President C. E. Taylor of Wake Forest College was strongly influential among the Baptists. Josiah William Bailey, editor of the Baptist *Biblical Recorder,* was throwing his fresh young energies and talent into the fight. These two powerful church groups had now developed confidence and momentum and were determined to clinch a victory over the State aid principle for higher education. They pushed the fight in the whole sectarian press and from every pulpit. Godly people should not be taxed to support and supply godless education. Higher education could not be "higher" unless it contained a distinctive religious element; and the State was estopped by the Constitution from giving religious instruction. Elementary education was a rightful field of the State; beyond this it should

---

5. To $20,000 for the University in 1895-96; $25,000 in 1896-97, and 1897-98. At this figure it stood when the Republican regime ended in 1900. See Treasurer's Report for these years, pp. 18-26.

not go. Jealousy over patronage was still at the core of the whole controversy, though glossed over by the sectarian leaders with arguments about types of education. The movement to hamstring the University was definitely coming to a head in the decade of the nineties. President Winston, not lacking a clear-eyed perspective of the formidable threat, proved a better strategist than any of his opponents. He successfully lined up the whole secular press and inspired prominent laymen to enter the lists as champions of freedom of the State from clerical control. He planted in the public mind the strong insinuation that the Baptist college, Wake Forest, through its endowment fund, was a sycophant of the Standard Oil Trust, and that Trinity, of the Methodists, was on its knees to the American Tobacco Trust of the Dukes.[6] His chief skill was shown as legislative lobbyist, where his talents as logician, as expositor of the theory of state education free from clerical control enabled him to exert great weight. The State Superintendent of Public Instruction, C. H. Mebane, a product of the Republican regime, had lined up with the church leaders and was exerting an influence reflecting the will of Kilgo and Bailey, whose cue had been to champion larger common school funds and withdrawal of support from the University at one and the same time. Winston bore in on the claim that the University's first concern was the health and advance of the common school system, of which it was the capstone. Here he was entirely sincere, knowing well that the University's whole future for patronage and opportunity rested upon advance of education among the masses of the people. He secured the advantage arising from the false position of the clericals, who held that only a modicum of the masses would need or benefit by higher education and that of a sort the church schools could best supply—since the end of education in its higher forms was to produce Christian leadership. Kilgo, in his paper the *Christian Educator,* founded at Trinity, had constantly stressed this point. Implication was clear that education for the masses beyond a moderate degree was not the goal of a sound system. Winston and Alderman held the door open to all whose capacities and endowments could be increased

6. See Luther L. Gobbel, *Church-State Relationships in Education in North Carolina,* Duke University Press, 1938, Chap. IV, p. 167.

by free opportunity. And theirs represented the drift of popular gropings about the whole subject of education, gropings that ultimately gathered coherence and then the momentum of a tide in popular feeling. This was Winston's and Alderman's fundamental advantage, for, in a popular democracy, whatever leadership places itself in harmony with the strongest underground swells, rides out all lesser currents and forces. Thus these two men rode the tides of rising forces. Winston, with his skill as a tactician, and Alderman, with his urbanity, ultimately isolated the enemy of State support to its University. By 1897 the battle was won.[7] Kilgo and Bailey were discomfited and checked. Kilgo was to go on, drawing Trinity College closer and closer to the source of its prosperity, the patronage of the Dukes of Durham. Kilgo went on to a bishopric, the fulfillment of his ambition; Trinity went on to transformation by Duke millions into Duke University, became a liberal institution of high quality, quite free from denominational restrictions or hampering jealousies. Today it is sought by ever-increasing numbers for the great intellectual opportunities it offers, rather than for the type of "Christian education" that marked the concept of its last clerical head. Also today Duke University, the child of an industrial fortune, and the University of North Carolina, child of the State, work in harmony and cooperation at the tasks that are common to all universities which would serve their day. Wake Forest, too, has long since sloughed off the spirit of jealousy, has rid itself of narrow ecclesiasticism, and now stands on a basis of solid achievement of a very high order in the collegiate world. Liberal heads for three successive administrations have guided its fortunes and established its repute, a repute now quite independent of clerical flavor.

President Winston, after five years of strenuous administration, critical years in which the fate of the University was really at stake, saw clear victory in sight. With plenty of self-confidence, his egoism nevertheless did not extend to a conviction that no other man could carry on from where he now was ready to leave off. There was Alderman, already in the faculty, already well prepared to take up the headship and draw enthusiastic support to himself and to the University. The offer of the head-

7. Gobbel, p. 168.

ship of the University of Texas seemed to Winston in 1896 an alluring prospect for the exercise of his talents, in a state less conservative, ready for pioneering, richer than North Carolina, and now anxious to stretch its limbs. He was quite earthy enough also to weigh the important material aspects of the offer, what with the needs of a family that peculiarly needed material protection. Two thousand and five hundred dollars was his stipend at the University of North Carolina, a princely sum among salaries in the State in his time. But this was doubled at Texas, luring Winston's acceptance. His career in Texas was short, a period of three years (1896-99). Leaving Carolina with great expectations of doing pioneer work in a young state university (organized in 1883) with a high endowment in public lands (2,000,000 acres) he conceived of his job as one of foundation building. Always self-confident and bold, he would set precedents and shape processes out of his own conceptions of the needful thing. He thought of Texas as a pioneer and unformed state in social evolution, and he illustrated something of the zeal of the missionary in education. Texas was sensitive and thought of herself as beyond the pioneer stage. Winston's platform capacity, highly effective in the State where it had been developed, was a bit too polished and out of tune to Texas tastes. The brand of speech exemplified in William Cowper Brann, editor of the *Iconoclast* at Waco, was more nearly the style to stir Texans of the period than the more self-controlled and polished platform style of the Carolinian.

Winston, in the assured confidence of his own judgment of men and measures, was also inclined to the arbitrary in his zeal to correct situations not to his liking. This had cropped out in his administration at Carolina, where he had stirred up strong student resentment by what was regarded as high-handed action in regard to athletics and certain cognate issues, mainly disciplinary, growing out of this interest. Old students of the time and citizens of the village will remember awakening to the sight of "Winston's Military Academy" painted in vermilion-colored letters two feet high across the face of Gerrard Hall, the Chapel of the time and center of all public activities. Promptly painted over by Winston's order these letters, now fifty years later, can be dimly seen through the successive coats of paint the building has meanwhile received. No suggestion is here made that this small episode colored the fundamental appraisal of Winston's able services to the University of his State. That appraisal rests upon the known sound administration he gave, plus his skill in fending against foes of the institution and the final commitment of the mind of the State to make its University a definite and primary interest. Winston's trend to the arbitrary nevertheless was a personal characteristic that he never sloughed off.

In Texas this arbitrariness gave trouble in the form of insecurity of tenure on the part of the faculty after an instance or so of a faculty member's even being dropped without notice or argument. Personal enmities were created that weakened his position. The Board of Regents, a small body of eight men, were soon not solid in his support. Hence Winston deemed that his advantage lay in a return to his native State, where a vacancy had just occurred in the presidency of the North Carolina College of Agriculture and Mechanic Arts at Raleigh and was opened to him. This position, less important in the collegiate world than either he had recently held, was not without possibilities for effective service. With his accustomed energy and purposefulness he advanced the organizational side of the Agricultural and Mechanical College and increased its student body, accomplishing this without any practical knowledge of either agricultural or mechanic arts. His old skill of bold representation was brought to bear on the legislature, resulting in very liberal (for the time) increase of appropriations and consequent large increase in equipment and in the faculty.

When Winston retired in 1908 on a Carnegie pension, he was still comparatively young (fifty-six) and with his health and vigor still unimpaired. He still commanded the confidence of his Board of Trustees and the patrons of the institution. But his tastes were those of the scholar, particularly of the classics, though he preserved a lively interest in subjects as far removed from each other as astronomy and anthropology. He desired a life of freedom from the administrative responsibility, a long period of relaxation which he could devote to urban contacts and travel abroad. This he was able to achieve, dividing his time between London and New York, and sometimes in the mountains of North Carolina. He watched the passing scene in state, nation, and the world with an eye of understanding, sharp in his criticisms of men and measures he did not approve, though never degenerating into a scold.

He retained a great optimism even as he grew old, marred only by hurts arising out of disasters to members of his family. These were of a sort particularly harassing, both his charming wife and his lovely daughter passing prematurely into the shadows of mental eclipse. His eldest and most brilliant son, too, after a rapid climb in the U. S. Navy to the rank of Commander, became mentally aberrant and failed in self-discipline, thus aborting a career of unusual promise. These things daunted but did not crush the vivid spirit of George Tayloe Winston. He retained a measure of buoyant philosophy and when his own strong physical equipment began to break up, with a true homing instinct for the place and scenes of his longest labors (1875-96), he retired to Chapel Hill for his last years, welcoming all the new evidences he found there of a vigorous and upthrusting life to which he had contributed in its formative period. Here he died in 1932 so quietly that the stream of the University world, now rushing on, was scarcely aware.

6

THE ADMINISTRATION OF EDWIN ANDERSON ALDERMAN

EDWIN ANDERSON ALDERMAN, who succeeded Winston in 1896, was of the Class of 1882 in the Battle years of the University. Born at the very opening of the Civil War in the seaport town of Wilmington, his ancestry was mainly English-Scotch agricultural and business settlers in the lower Cape Fear country where they had been planted for several generations before Alderman was born. Alderman's biographer, Dumas Malone,[1] ascribes much of the qualities of his subject to his mother, a not unusual convention often in harmony with fact.

This mother was a Cobbett, probably of Irish origin, and possessed of both a wit and a purposefulness that distinguished her among her neighbors and friends. She loved contacts and conversation and had strong convictions that the spoken word was an instrument of influence and power. This idea seems certainly to have taken early hold on the son, was developed by him as a college student, and undoubtedly became the source of the early confidence in himself that flowered into his remarkable career as orator and educational statesman. Inherent in him also was a convinced spirit of democracy, a belief in the virtues and capacities of the average man and his right to equal opportunity as the keystone of a sound order and the hope of the future. This idea was basic in all his future labors—the realization of a democracy uplifted by popular education to a point where all its energies would be released. At the same time, and coloring his concept of an educated democracy, were the virtues of gentility in manners, speech, and action in all the relations of men. In a peculiar sense, as his career unfolded, he became the embodiment

---

1. *Edwin A. Alderman, A Biography*, by Dumas Malone, published in 1940, is a full-length portrait of his subject, written with considerable objectivity though colored in spots by the author's warm admiration.

in his person of this marriage of gentility and an educated democracy. Nor was the union artificial, even though from the first there was some suspicion that the qualities of natural gentility so apparent in his person, his dress, his manners, and his speech were hall-marks of forms of another day, a day in which gentility gave special claims to special place and advantage to the few.

It was fortunate for North Carolina, for the South, and ultimately for the nation that Alderman, with his particular talents, as yet only mildly indicated, should have chosen deliberately to make his career in public education rather than in the law, which seems to have tempted him as he passed out of college. He had passed through the State University in its years of crude poverty and struggle for survival under Battle. There he had been influenced by Battle, by George T. Winston, his Latin and English teacher, who was later Battle's successor and his own predecessor in the presidency. Ralph H. Graves, professor of engineering and astronomy, a cultivated gentleman of the finer sort, and Francis P. Venable, Alderman's own successor as president, seem to have been the other faculty members most generous in their contributions which molded from above.

In the student body Alderman found a wide satisfaction in his contacts, and hammered out binding ties with a series of his contemporaries who in after life were greatly to influence his career, either as wise, understanding, and applauding friends or as team mates, mostly these, in the great purpose of popular education with which his name and theirs were soon to become inseparably linked. This list of college friends, not exclusive, contained a group of real personalities, among them M. C. S. Noble, Frank B. Dancy, R. W. Winston, Charles B. Aycock, Locke Craig, James Y. Joyner, and Charles D. McIver. Four of these men, Noble, Aycock, Joyner, and McIver were each to impinge in an important way upon the educational awakening that began in the nineties and proceeded to a climax following the turn of the century. Alderman and McIver particularly stood in the forefront of the movement and came to embody its purposes and ideals. Drawn down to their simplest meaning, the doctrines of these two men sum up to the claim that every human being has the same right to be educated that he has to be free, and that it is the obligation of the State to provide the opportunity. This simple formula, now so generally accepted, was well-nigh revolutionary in North Carolina in its nineteenth-century poverty, and the man was bold who would stake his career upon its acceptance by the State.

Nor did Alderman or McIver spring into the arena fully armed immediately upon their emergence from college. A seven-year apprenticeship at teaching under the guidance of Edward P. Moses at Goldsboro, where the latter was striving with skill and persistence to build up a city school, municipally supported, served as an incubation period. A visit from J. L. M. Curry, drawn by Moses to boost his popular campaign, doubtless confirmed Alderman in the faith. Moses was called to Raleigh in 1885 to do for the captial what he had done for Goldsboro, and Alderman was adjudged qualified for the succession. Administrative duties first fell to him in Goldsboro, made somewhat easier to fit his shoulders by the fact that Charles B. Aycock, lawyer in the town, was chairman of his board of trustees. Aycock was, at the same time and place, germinating the ideas and convictions that brought him to the official forefront of the educational movement in his election as governor of the State in 1900. Here he translated the doctrine of free eduction into political action, laying the foundations of North Carolina's rise from the lowly position she had so long occupied in the galaxy of American states.

Moses at Raleigh kept his eye on Alderman as his favorite protégé and was doubtless influential in Alderman's selection (1889) by the State Board of Education as an agent of the board for effecting a campaign to stir popular sentiment in support of public education. McIver was associated with him in the task, and the institute method was fixed upon by them as promising the greatest results. Preliminary preparation by local support in the counties of the State was to provide a week of contact in each county where the institute conductor was to instruct and stimulate local teachers and at the same time bring home to the public in attendance the great need and advantage of enlarged public interest and financial support of a vital system of public education. The whole procedure might well have been a flash in the pan, a gesture without results, had it not been for the fortunate choice of the two young men, both of whom had a flair for the platform and public contacts. More important still, both had a burning zeal to be effective instruments in awakening the people to their greatest need. Both were yet immature in age and experience, but both were confident in their convictions. Alderman, particularly, had already attracted attention, first in college and later in local appearances, as an unusually attractive speaker—in respect both to the substance of his thought and particularly to his promising platform artistry.

His and McIver's tours of the State as institute conductors continued over a period of two and one-half years, in the meantime achieving such popular interest in their objectives that other educational enthusiasts were brought into the field. Noble, Moses, J. Y. Joyner, Alexander Graham, and J. J. Blair—all superintendents of successful city schools which were largely products of their skill and enthusiasm—were added to the work that Alderman and McIver had launched. The thing amounted to a strong, deep-stirring popular impulse for popular education and represented a landmark in the history of the State even though so quickly covered over after its inception by the political and social turmoil that characterized the decade of the nineties in North Carolina history.

McIver's thought and feeling all through his participation in this unique campaign was particularly concerned with the obligation of the State to interest itself in the education of its women. Swift success was the outcome, the first apparent fruitage of the now really popular education movement. The State legislature made provision in 1891 for a normal college for women at Greensboro, and McIver was naturally named as its head. It might easily have been thought, at a much later day, that the launching of the State's effort at higher education for women ought to have taken the form of increased appropriations for the University and women's admission there, thus saving the cost of an additional plant and separate organization and administration and duplication of effort. This, in recent years, furnished the main argument in the movement for consolidation that has now taken place. Advocates of this view, that there was failure in educational statesmanship in not developing the long view, fail to take into consideration social outlooks of the period, or to distinguish the practical from the impractical. The social organism, being a living thing, is unpredictable in respect to its future, in the direction it will take. The position of women was changing and advancing in the whole last half of the nineteenth century, but only a fanatic or extreme visionary would have foretold the changes in their traditional relationship that have taken place in the past forty years.

When the normal school for women was founded at Greensboro there was as yet no demand for coeducation of the sexes. The founding itself marked a great advance in the rights of women to consideration by the political state, an advance largely the product of McIver's energy and views, shared by Alderman and most of the other members of the "institute" group in the early nineties. Even so, their most potent arguments had to turn on the need of educated teachers in the public schools, and a large majority of these were women. True, McIver struck deeper, emphasizing intelligent motherhood as perhaps the greatest social need. There was great potency in the argument, and it continued to grow to enormous weight, but the practical and most effective argument to the political-minded was the need to prepare teachers. Thus for quite a long period after the normal school was founded it was thought of as for that paramount purpose. To prepare women for other careers, to open a wide door to general enlightenment except as it bore upon teaching and motherhood was as yet beyond the scope of the State's social purpose. In the State's concept of its University there was no restricting limitation, no particular commitment to one form of education above another. Certainly this had been so since the loss of the Land Grant Fund and the emergence of the Agricultural and Mechanical College at Raleigh. Thus the University was in freer position for future development into a real University than if it had retained the Land Grant Fund and had constantly been held chargeable for turning out farmers and mechanics on an appreciable and growing scale. So likewise it could not have strengthened itself in the early nineties by contending for coeducation of women at Chapel Hill prior to much further advance in the Woman's Movement. It is true that at the end of another decade a narrow door was opened to a few women students, largely through Alderman's influence. Even so the crack was so narrow, so few women seeped through that the innovation went largely unobserved by the State. Nor was the breach in tradition popular among the students at Chapel Hill, where women students, very few in numbers, long remained an anomaly upon the campus and in a classroom. While the students were hostile or mildly contemptuous, the faculty was apparently indifferent.

The act of the legislature for the establishment of the Normal and Industrial School for women came in the midst of McIver's and Alderman's work as institute conductors and was largely the product of their efforts. In their reports to the State Superintendent of Public Instruction while on their circuits of the State they had, in agreement, strongly stressed the need. They had joined in memorials to the legislature[2] outlining a plan and urging its adoption. The act was perfected February 18, 1891, and the school was opened in October, 1892, McIver having been elected president and Alderman appointed professor of literature and history. The institution was immediately off to a fair start with 200 students the very first year, with these two ardent enthusiasts shaping its foundations. McIver gave the rest of his life (d. 1906) to building up and expanding the influence of this sound institution, a labor of great love and pride. Alderman, after one year, was caught in the net of the astute George Tayloe Winston and brought to Chapel Hill as professor of the history and philosophy of education. McIver filled the vacancy at Greensboro with James Yadkin Joyner, a fortunate choice for the future of the school. Joyner had been closely associated with McIver and Alderman in their second year of institute work. Alderman was brought to the University to fill a new chair, a department for the training of teachers, and to cultivate a "more intimate and practical connection with the school system of the state."[3] The choice could not have been more propitious because of Alderman's leadership in the current public education movement and the wide contacts he had already made in the State. He carried with him, therefore, a popular approval that no other person at that time could

2. Compare Malone's *Life of Alderman*. See Scrapbook, Normal and Industrial College, Vol. I, 1891-93.

3. Malone, *Life of Alderman*, pp. 54-55, quoting Trustee Records of the University of North Carolina, 1891-98, pp. 264 ff.

have commanded. And, as Malone points out, and as Winston knew, popular approval was a valuable asset in view of the fact that the future of the University was hardly yet assured, North Carolina's hardly yet having made up its mind to the permanency of state support of higher education in a state-supported University. Moreover it was just at this time that the denominational hostility was being renewed in its last grand assault upon the principal. Winston was to stand up to the fight, offering no quarter, but the presence of the popular Alderman in the faculty, representing as he did a practical link between the University and the public school and high school interest, gave Winston confidence in the ultimate outcome.

Alderman immediately revived at Chapel Hill a summer school for teachers, an activity that had been closed since 1884 by the withdrawal of the small appropriation of $2000 it had existed on during the eight years of its life. Dr. Battle, in the chair of history, where he was to remain until 1907, was greatly heartened at the restoration of the summer school, for he had always held that its earlier existence had brought the University into highly valuable relations with public education and made the public University-conscious. Now that so admirable and fitting a choice as Alderman was to head it, there was every prospect of its effective continuous life.[4] In this he was right in that within a few years, what with this lasting link with the public school interest and an increasing volume of alumni turned out, the University was now floating into safer waters.

During the three years of Alderman's professorship before he became president in succession to Winston in 1896, he touched the life of the University in a vital way other than the revival of the summer school. This grew out of his vision of the place and importance of library facilities in the life of an educational institution. He became faculty supervisor of the library. He gave to this supervision more than formal quality. He wrote on the subject in the recently established *Alumni Quarterly*,[5] giving pointed and definite expression to ideas quite in advance of his

---

4. Battle, *History of the University of North Carolina*, Vol. II, pp. 504, 505, 526.

5. October, 1894, pp. 10-14.

time. "The library," he pointed out, "should be co-equal with chairs of instruction, bearing a relation to humanistic studies comparable with that of laboratories to the natural sciences." A proper library, he held, was not only a storehouse of thought, but a laboratory, a workshop, a mine, an inspiration for both professors and students.[6] In sum total it is not too much to say that Alderman's influence in the University on library development gave the initial push that gathered increasing momentum until the University Library became the heart of the institution as a really great educational center.

Manner and manners played a not inconsiderable part in the increasing reputation Alderman had made in the State. This was equally true of this period as professor at the University and then as president. Whether or not his bearing and his perfection of manners were a matter of cultivation or a natural endowment may perhaps be subject to debate, though there is abundant evidence that this quality of urbanity and good form adhered to him when he first came to Chapel Hill as a student at the age of seventeen years. Possessed of a handsome and naturally graceful physical appearance, gifted beyond the average in good taste about clothes, Alderman gave the impression of a man of rare charm. With an ingrained conviction of social democracy, believing in the worth of the common man, he set a standard of good taste for the common man that was a contribution of no mean sort in a rural democracy where poverty and the breakup of an old social order had tended to coarsen manners. Nor were Alderman's manners a nostalgic reflection of a past day, for preeminently he was a man of the new South, a South striving to meet a new day along new lines of endeavor.

Alderman's special genius lay in platform performance, a gift he had cultivated from one success to another from his college days onward. The linking together of apt and pleasing phrases, the playing on popular emotions easily stirred were not the essence of his oratory. There was a content in what he said, the product of wisdom gleaned from wide and continuous reading coupled with a gift for discriminating interpretation and selection. These set up his own thought processes, which reached conclusions that

6. Malone, *Life of Alderman*, p. 60.

were his own. Sure of his conclusions, though without dogmatism, he presented his thoughts to audiences not only with a perfect speaking voice, and adorned with the apt phrases and flashes of genuine wit, but with an organized continuity of meaning that drew his words home. He lived to administer and invigorate three universities before his life closed in 1931, but all the while the chief sum of his influence on his own state, on the South, and, finally, on the nation, derived from his ideas on education expressed from the platform.

Alderman was inaugurated as president of the University of North Carolina January 27, 1897, having been chosen unanimously by the Board of Trustees in the preceding August to succeed Winston, who had accepted the presidency of the University of Texas. He was the natural choice for the trustees to make in the then circumstances of the institution. Young (thirty-five), fresh, vivid, and purposeful he was, by virtue of his identity with and leadership of the public education movement during the past five years, more widely known in the State than any other man in the faculty. This was true despite the fact that there were a number of very able men in the small faculty of sixteen at the time of Alderman's selection for the presidency. But these were, at the time, identified with their special fields of interest, building up their particular departments, laying strong foundations for the University's internal structure, and were scarcely known to the State at large. All of them had been gathered by either Battle or Winston; nearly all of them were to remain for a lifetime of service to the institution, in the meantime not only giving breadth and permanence to their individual fields of instruction, but communicating to the place a spirit of scholarship, its dignity and its worth. At the moment there was nearly an equal balance between the chairs in the sciences and the humanities, but with the greater present and potential energy represented by the men of science, including Venable, H. V. Wilson, and Collier Cobb.

None of this faculty manifested any resentment at the elevation of Alderman, so recent a recruit to their numbers, so much their junior in degrees and academic experience. Alderman had tact of the first order and the ability to work with men without creating jealousy. His sound confidence in himself never took the form of underrating others. Moreover his self-confidence at this stage was based largely on his pre-eminent success in gaining and holding the interest and leadership of all the rising forces which were awakening to the educational needs of the State and demanding advance. The old faculty that Alderman now headed knew that he had the attention, as no other had, of the educational impulse of the State just now beginning to stir with new life, that he had largely contributed to this impulse, very nearly representing its main spring. This was the strength of the man in the University internally and externally, and in a yet critical time of its fortunes. Though Battle and Winston had made steady progress in pushing down the roots of the institution, the winds raging about the tops of the tree were still nearly in balance with its grip on life. The denominational interests had regathered vitality and were making what proved to be their last real threat. Kilgo and Bailey were at the zenith of their attack upon the principle of the State's right to furnish higher educational facilities out of taxpayers' money. The diplomatic Winston, with energy and shrewd strategy, had lost no ground to the University's opponents, rather he had made gains, but the corner had not yet been wholly turned. Alderman, with his urbanity and polish, his assumption and insistence that the University was the integral head and crown of the public school system the State was under obligation to build, soon scuttled the forces of the opposition. "The University," he proclaimed, "is the people's school. Her watchword and her graven motto shall be creative energy, enlightened civilization and untrammeled manhood."[7]

Alderman's induction into the presidency of the University came at a very critical time for other reasons than the renewed onslaught of the sectarian leaders. It was a critical political year in the nation and in the State. The Democratic party was now thrusting for a monetary revolution under its new-found leader, W. J. Bryan. The "hard times" of the preceding Cleveland ad-

---

7. From his Inaugural Address, January 27, 1897. Vol. I, No. 2. The University *Record*. The University *Record,* so continuously useful to the institution from this date on, had just been founded, the first number appearing in December, 1896.

ministration were looking for a cure in monetary inflation and there was large unrest in the nation. Alderman had assumed his duties as president of the University in September, 1896, but his formal inauguration had been deferred to January, 1897, out of deference to the preoccupation of the public with political matters in the fall of 1896. In the State, too, a political overturn had just been recorded in the preceding election. The Republicans and agrarians (Populists) in fusion had now captured both legislative and executive control of the State, after twenty years of Democratic supremacy following the overthrow of Reconstruction. This twenty years of Democratic party supremacy had been one of caution, of ultra-conservatism, of feeding on resentments and sectional issues to the neglect of progressive measures in the interest of the masses. In harmony with the general Southern regional pattern, this period has been labeled the era of the Bourbons. Chief fear of the Bourbons arose out of the unsettled issue of the Negro in politics, a troubled question at the very heart of the life of the whole South. This issue, temporarily settled by the Southern states' constitutional amendments around the end of the decade of the nineties, in North Carolina became involved with the agrarian unrest that had produced the Populist party. This party, hoping to attain some of its ends in the overthrow of the Bourbons in State politics, had combined with the State Republican party in 1896 and the fusion had resulted in a four-year supremacy for the combination. [The manuscript stops abruptly here.—Editor.]

7

THE ADMINISTRATION OF FRANCIS PRESTON VENABLE

ON THE RESIGNATION OF E. A. Alderman to go to Tulane in 1900, Dr. F. P. Venable was chosen by the Board of Trustees to assume the presidency. The trustee minutes disclose no rival candidate and the election was by unanimous choice. Venable had been in the faculty since 1880 as professor of chemistry. He was by birth a Virginian, was a graduate from the university of that state, where his father, Charles Scott Venable, was professor of mathematics and chairman of the faculty. The elder Venable had been a member of General Lee's staff during the Civil War and a representative of that element of Virginia gentlemen who so long preserved much of English tradition and gave so notable a priority to their state in influence upon our national life and the shape of its institutions.

The influence of Virginia, that is to say, Virginians, upon the history of our Republic has been of fundamental importance in the shape and direction our history has taken. Caught up in the vortex of the national explosion of 1861 produced by irreconcilable trends in economic and social sectionalism, Virginia, by virtue of the verdict of war, lost her pre-eminence in the sisterhood of states without losing her soul. Rising again from her ashes would be a work of time. Hope lay in the quality of her sons, in their powers of readjustment, and in reconstruction along the lines of their English traditions.

The young Dr. F. P. Venable came to the University of North Carolina as a scientist at a time when all the spade work in the sciences had yet to be done, at least in our region. The turn of his mind was toward research—investigation that would produce and multiply the advantages of man over the nature of matter. By dint of his great industry, his capacities as a very able chemist rapidly unfolded during the twenty years of service to the University before he became its president. Under the successive administrations of Battle, Winston, and Alderman he, along with Henry Van Peters Wilson, began to make the University known as a place where important advances in science were taking shape. He published in the scientific journals of the nation; he wrote textbooks on chemistry. His analytical mind and his great physical drive were producing results in and outside the unfolding college. His balance of mind and skill at organization set forces in motion with profound after-effects upon the life of the institution. He was the main originator of the Elisha Mitchell Scientific Society, was its first president and guided its early direction into paths that have made this society, with its *Journal*, a notable voice in the advance of science for the last half century. He recognized the need of a printing establishment for University use. Though no funds were available for the purpose, he, in association with several of his colleagues, set in being a University Press as a private enterprise, without hope or aim of personal gain. This University Press was a mere print shop for quite a number of years, but proved so useful and advantageous to University interest that it was acquired by the University. It planted the press idea that later blossomed into the University of North Carolina Press of the present day, without which the University would be shorn of one of its fairest characteristics as a potent force in the world of learning. Venable, likewise, fully appreciated the value of the University *Record* established by Alderman, and gave it its place as a continuing journal that has preserved the picture of so many facts, so many activities, and so many of the faces of men, that it is an abiding record of the life of the University.

Thus Venable was a practical man, both in his science and in the material shaping of the University structure in its formative period. He stinted his energies in no way, but gave full service to all efforts looking to the welfare of the institution. No man, president or professor, during the twenty years of his service before he became president in 1900, gave more generously and wisely of himself than did Venable. The facile, shrewd, and fighting Winston, the polished, genteel, and cultivated Alderman may each in his turn have been the wisest choices in their respective periods for the presidency in the ten years before Venable came in: Winston because of his political-mindedness and his capacity as a strategist in warfare with strong enemies of the University, primarily the sectarian leaders out for the very life of the University; Alderman because of his disarming blandness, and his symbolism of the rising tide of democratic zeal for dissipating the clouds that hung over public education in the State and the region.

Venable was beneficiary of the contributions of both these administrations when he followed the ten years which compassed them both. But inside the University in that period, the University that Winston and Alderman were selling the State would have been a lesser thing by far except for the toil of Venable.

There have been not a few instances where scientists, by virtue of unusual reputation built in their specific fields, have been called out of their laboratory to head the executive administration of the institution in which they worked. Yet a scientist may, or may not, be an effective administrator. Besides, there may be entailed a most considerable loss to science in the necessary diversion to administrative tasks. Administration, particularly in a state university like ours, dependent for its life-blood upon popular and legislative favor, ordinarily profits best with a head sufficiently political-minded to translate to the state the conception of values its university is. This in itself is a huge task.

Dr. Venable himself, always primarily a scientist in the field of chemistry, lagged not at all in this interest when he became president of the University. He was still an habitué of his laboratory when administrative burdens allowed, still kept up a small amount of teaching of advanced chemistry, and occasionally published results of his research. Nevertheless and necessarily, the burdens of his administrative post were heavy, and he sensed the opportunity arriving at the turn of the century for an expanded University and its entry upon wider usefulness. For using this opportunity Venable was ready. Already, despite his immersion in research and teaching during his past twenty years, he had become a prop and aid to each successive president, Battle, Winston, and Alderman, in the solution of the practical problems which the University had had to solve in its fight for the right to exist and to grow. His hand was in most of these solutions, not because he willed to share in them, or was ambitious to participate in them for any priority to be derived, but because each president in turn, looking over his faculty for available aid, found in Venable rare practical common sense along with his ever-growing eminence as a scientist. Thus without any thought of grooming for the presidency he was not only prepared for it when Alderman departed for Tulane in 1900, but had been so for at least the past ten years. Yet it is more than probable that within that time Venable never thought of the presidency in terms of self. He was developing his science, creating a reputable department of research, gathering a few well-trained young men about him and tying up his University with the unfolding scientific progress of the country. Administrative aid and counsel he furnished as an extra and out of the abundance of his energies, mental and physical.

Venable assumed the presidency at a moment in some particulars fortunate. The twenty-five years since the University's revival had all been critical years. Battle's primary contribution had been to fan a spark into a bit of flame, to defend it against the adverse winds of political unsettlement and convince the State it had a right to live. Winston had come on in time to weather out the attack of the church schools and the denominational onslaught. His D'Artagnan-like rapier, backed by the keenest intelligence and an adroit strategy, had forced the sectarians to take cover even when led by the slaughter-minded Kilgo and his companion-in-arms, Josiah William Bailey. Then had come Alderman with his urbanity and friendliness, representing the victory of the public school idea with a liberal state university to cap the edifice of popular enlightenment. Alderman's humor and gentility had helped to put out the last fires of the controversy with the sectarians which Winston had smothered. Thus the University had lived, though it had lived in poverty, poverty not of the spirit but of the financial resources that an impoverished State had yet to deny.

Venable on coming to office knew that financial resources must be increased, and that right early, if the University should have a chance to do its work for the State. He knew the period of dire State poverty since the reopening in 1875, and had learned the lessons of strict economy. Nevertheless, he believed that the time had now arrived for greater confidence in the future, that our poverty complex should be thrown off. A new fertility of the spirit, inculcated at the University, could accomplish this in considerable part if the resources could be induced from the State. He did not contemn the worth of private gifts, but he thought of these as possible incidentals and in no sense a substitution for an increasing subsidy from the State whose institution it was. Put in more capital, was his creed, and returns will be had in greater proportion than the investment. He had never known the State to appropriate to the University a larger sum than $25,000 and that was at the end of Alderman's preceding administration.

There were several favoring circumstances that made the period of Venable's administration propitious for the University's prospects. One was a slow but rising tide of state rehabilitation in matters economic. Manufacturing industries were invading the State and becoming important, particularly the processing of cotton and tobacco, the two outstanding agricultural products of the region. Very early in the nineteenth century there had been an impulse in the State toward cotton processing. Certain long-headed entrepreneurs like the Holts and the Battles had established modest cotton mills in the second decade of the century. These, and a few others that had come early into being, were kept alive through the remainder of the century despite the economic vicissitudes of the whole Southern region and the cataclysmic effect of Civil War, Reconstruction, and the poverty that followed. Tobacco manufacture of a modern type made a beginning only after the Civil War, but it held out prospects of profit to the industrial life of the State. Agriculture was beginning a slow improvement at the turn of the century, though it still lagged by virtue of nondiversification and continuing unsettlement in labor conditions. Also there were violent oscillations of product prices, which made agriculture everywhere in the South much of a gamble, even though it was as yet the chief hope for any economic ease for this section of the nation.

Even so, new economic energy was stirring and was reacting upon mental energy with definite promise of educational advances in North Carolina. Charles Brantley Aycock was just becoming governor of the State, a man of the people whose vision was toward the future rather than toward the past, and whose passion was for public education. His term of four years (1901-5) gave notable impetus to popular interest in an educated citizenry, to be achieved by new investment in schools from the lowest to the highest ranks. His influence was permanent in emphasis and has carried on until this day. The University felt it in definite effect, in increased appropriations for maintenance, and in expansion of plant and facilities at State expense. The registrants at the University nearly doubled in Venable's administration and annual appropriations rose in the period from $25,000 to $95,000.

This was not an adequate budget to carry out all that Venable hoped and planned for, but it was a proud advance and gave the president and his faculty confidence that a notable future lay ahead for the institution. New life-blood was beating in its veins. Space for the humanities and laboratories for the sciences were almost keeping pace with need. Faculty personnel were adjusted in number and quality to the new opportunity for service to the State. Over all, Venable was keen to induce and maintain the scientific spirit in the whole institution. In the humanities as well as in natural and applied science, research, ever more intensive, was the key that would unlock the door of the treasure house of knowledge, and knowledge and its sane use were the goals of man.

Venable grew into the conception, aided and stimulated by upcoming young talent in his faculty, notably by Louis Round Wilson, that a modern library was fundamental to an institution that would serve the purposes of its existence. A library, ever increasing in its store of the knowledge of the past, as well as of the present endeavors of scholars who were making brick for the rising edifice of human enlightenment, seemed to Venable and Wilson a prerequisite of an institution of learning.

In the present era this fact is axiomatic, but at the turn of the century it had had no great recognition at the University, or, if recognized, there had been such great lack of means and organizing ability that an adequate library and library facilities had not been worked out to take their due place in the demands of the faculty and the youths that came up to the University for instruction. The period of Venable saw this lack supplied. The moment was propitious on account of the rising appreciation of the need, and the opportunity presented by Andrew Carnegie's particular form of restoration to the public of much of the profits accruing from his Midas touch in industrial organization and exploitation. This resource was tapped for a generous gift, on the terms that it be matched in amount by the recipient—a wise provision in this form of philanthropy. The provision was met by the University through dignified appeal to alumni and friends, and a library building, as such, came into use in 1907, the middle year of Venable's term.

This library, then a notable acquisition, had a profound effect upon the University as a working institution, giving such impetus to the University as a library center that the new building was early outgrown. However, by that time the State was effectually sold on the library idea as a prerequisite of educational advance. Thus only twenty years later than the opening of the Carnegie Library, the State financed the present Library at a cost of $625,000.

The important thing about the history of the library in Venable's period of tenure was the growth of the concept in the University and in the State, particularly in the University, that a well-organized and well-equipped library was the soul of the institution, that without such an arsenal of materials, past and present, there could be no vivid and expanding life. Venable himself was neither wholly nor nearly wholly responsible for the rise of this idea. His mind had been so nearly absorbed in his science and in certain immediate practical problems of the institution before he became president, with these problems doubled when he became responsible head, that it is not to be wondered at that the old library limitations and shortcomings seemed more or less natural. His mind as an executive ran to the idea of a general balance in rounding out the muscles of the University. Expansion of the physical plant and facilities he saw as a first need, then a careful selection of an increased faculty personnel, and, imperatively, the maintenance and deeping of the scientific spirit in scholarship and research.

Fortunately the library idea tied in perfectly with all these objectives. More fortunately still, a young man was rising in the faculty group with unfolding and very modern ideas as to the place of the library in a modern educational institution. This man was Louis Round Wilson, a graduate of the University in 1899. Wilson had returned to the University for graduate study and to become librarian in 1901 by Venable's selection and appointment. The history of library development in North Carolina is to a very large degree the history of Wilson's activities, afterward extended to a much wider field than this University and State.

Venable's organizing impulse was felt throughout the University, covering other matters than increase of facilities in an expanded plant. A graduate school came into being in 1903 to meet the rising demand for advanced study and research. There had been some desultory offering in the University curriculum for advanced study leading to the Master of Arts degree, and a few doctorates had been awarded. Venable pushed on for a real beginning in graduate studies, believing that research in the sciences and the humanities was the hall-mark of a real university. Yet he did not disregard the fact that the history and tradition of his institution committed it first of all to sound undergraduate teaching. Here too he saw wide opportunity for better integration of courses, for clearer delineation of departments and fixing of responsibilities. In the matter of integration he unified the three undergraduate degrees, Bachelor of Arts, Bachelor of Science, and Bachelor of Philosophy, interrelating the courses of study so as to lead to the one uniform degree of Bachelor of Arts.

Venable's personality has been a subject of varied opinions. Some saw in him an over-rigid and stern addiction to duty, unrelieved by much of a sense of humor, a quality that his three predecessors had in marked degree, even though of different quality in each. Venable's sense of duty was markedly strong. He took his own problems seriously and liked to see the same attitude in others. This inclined him, as an administrator, to the principle of discipline. He had come up through the years of the University when its student clientele was rather raw and callow. He thought of the college, and himself in particular, as *in loco parentis* to the student body. Breaches in discipline and inattention to the routine of duty marred the character not only of the individual but of the whole University, for which he was responsible in the eyes of parents and of the State. Not that he wished to hold the natural ebullience of youth in a strait jacket, but that its energies should be turned in lawful and healthful directions. He was a strong advocate of athletics and encouraged all sports with his steady support. Yet he was pronouncedly opposed to venality in sports, to hired players, and to all that threatened the amateur quality of athletic activities in an educational institution. He thought of college sports as a healthful means to make better gentlemen out of those who engaged in them, and at the same time set a standard for non-participants. To opposing ideas and their advocates he was brusk and sometimes impatient. This bruskness was interpreted by some as proof of a domineering spirit. Yet no critic ever found in him a lack of true gentility. He was a gentleman by breeding and by innate feeling, and reflected this quality in all his contacts and in all his actions.

Venable's Presbyterian affiliation in religion never marked him out as a true heir of the inner spirit of real Calvinism. God might not err, but his children could and often did. It was the duty of man to seek the good and perchance he might find it, but all were not in error who did not find it in Venable's way. There has been much talk of the liberal tradition at the University, a tradition well worth preservation as long as tolerance remains a virtue. But real liberalism in matters of religion and social attitudes is a thing of the spirit, very different from wide gestures about "freedom and democracy" so current in a later time than Venable's.

Venable's relations with his faculty were possibly a bit formal, but always considerate and understanding. The faculty was increased rapidly in his period, but the older members of the group were men whom he had worked with during much of the period before he became president. Among these were Eben Alexander, Joshua W. Gore, ex-President K. P. Battle, R. H. Whitehead, Thomas Hume, H. V. Wilson, Collier Cobb, M. C. S. Noble, and Major Cain. All were close to Venable by virtue of their common service to the University in less propitious times. Some of these, notably Hume, Alexander, and Gore, were destined to pass during Venable's period. Also Mrs. Cornelia Phillips Spencer died in 1908. The deaths of these people in the course of nature left notable gaps in the University's stream of life, though Mrs.

Spencer, whose life had been entwined with the place for seventy years, had not been resident here since 1894. Yet her spirit had hovered in Chapel Hill, and still constitutes one of its treasured memories. Hume, Alexander, and Gore, each in his own way, had colored University life with great advantage to its culture. In the memories of alumni their removal seemed a real misfortune. Yet others of the old guard remained. Though Whitehead departed for Virginia, he was still neighbor and friend. But Battle, H. V. Wilson, Cobb, Noble, and Cain were yet long to remain, serving as a sort of core of the pre-century University, giving time for adjustment of the new men that Venable was calling into its service.

In expanding the faculty to meet the new needs and opportunities that the new century had presented, Venable proved notably capable in the selection of personnel. He looked first to the record of scientific training, and then to his judgment of capacity for adjustment and growth. Few executives are wholly unerring in the exercise of the function of appointment. Especially is this true of a university's head, the problem being the more complex by virtue of the varying facets of quality required, or at least needed, in a particular post.

To the uninitiated the role of a teacher seems quite simple: to have some "learning" in general, or in a particular field, and be able to "tell it" to "inquiring" youth. The initiated know this is only the bottom step of the stairs to be climbed by the effective scholar who essays to teach. Continuing growth in his own scholarship, attained only by ceaseless effort (compensated for by the satisfactions and consciousness of a fuller mental life); achievement of the art (if perchance he may) of superinducing the "inquiry" spirit where it sometimes does not exist; so appreciating the qualities that characterize "human culture" that he reflects them in all his contacts. Even these are only a few of the fundamentals of the teacher's role, a role exercised normally in an atmosphere of swirling cross-currents as to where chief emphasis belongs, of changing factions and needs of a self-conscious democracy.

Venable, in filling in the gaps left by deaths or departures, and in expanding the staff to meet new requirements, was singularly judicious in the choice of men. Probably for the first time since the reopening in 1875 was the president free to make choices without regard to religious or political coloration of the men selected. Battle had had to walk a tight rope in both these realms; Winston and Alderman scarcely less so, though in Alderman's administration the tension was relaxing. But with the turn of the century, as Venable came in, the Democratic party seemed assured of supremacy, and nervousness and fears died down on the issue of the University's survival. The party could and would protect the institution and seemed inclined to make it free, free to perform its destined functions.

At the same time, by fortunate circumstance as well as by the long defense that Battle, Winston, and Alderman had made against the sectarians, the fruit of toleration began to ripen. Kilgo and Bailey and the forces they had represented were moving toward increasing impotence in their old purpose of cutting at the very life of the University by moving the people to deny State aid. The old asperities of the sects were dying, even though slowly and reluctantly.

All this was very fortunate for Venable's administration. Nonpolitical minded to a remarkable degree and with the true scientist's outlook on sectarian intolerance he would have been greatly discomfited in an atmosphere lacking the essentials of freedom in academic thought. Therefore, Venable concerned himself not at all with the religious or political affiliation of his selectees for appointments. At the present day, only thirty years since the end of his administration, such practice seems so axiomatic and natural that it tends to illustrate the rapidity of pace in social evolution in our times.

Even a partial list of Venable's additions to the faculty staff is a roster of notable quality in scholarship, in investigation, in productive literature and scientific conquests, in administrative development. It discloses the fact that the University was no longer a parochial institution of mere college grade among others of its kind, but was in reality a University, where intellectual horizons were being lifted and static frontiers destroyed. Regional priority was in near grasp, despite the still slender budget the State could allow, and national ranking was soon in sight. This was largely due to Venable's selection of men. The process was as interesting as were its results. Venable's budgets rarely allowed him to look over the national field of scholars and induce men with already established large reputations to come to his University. His recruitments out of this group are fairly meagre, represented chiefly by Charles Alphonso Smith, brought in in 1902 in English language and literature and soon to head the revitalized graduate school; Lucius Polk McGehee to head the Law School; Charles W. Bain in Greek to succeed Eben Alexander, who died in 1910; and A. H. Patterson, in Physics.

Venable's policy, encouraged by his budget limitations, was to add younger men with vital qualities and pronounced ambitions in their respective fields. These he would encourage and support, give as free hand as his means allowed, and watch their qualities unfold. There is no period of equal length in the University's post-bellum history in which so many men of the University's staff laid the foundations and got underway the structure of professional careers that not only made them eminent in their own University, but in the arts and sciences beyond its boundaries. In this group, though not complete as here given, were George Howe, Latin; William Chambers Coker, botany; Harry Woodburn Chase, philosophy of education; Edward Kidder Graham, English; J. G. deRoulhac Hamilton, history; Charles Holmes Herty and J. E. Mills, chemistry; Louis Round Wilson, library; William Morton Dey, romance languages; Nathan Wilson Walker, education; James E. Latta, physics; and Marvin Hendrix Stacy, mathematics. Archibald Henderson, in mathematics; W. de B. MacNider, in biology; Latta, in physics; and Graham, in English, had been added in 1898 and 1899 under Alderman, but were given permanent appointment under Venable.

Six of these men died in the midst of notable careers in their fields, Graham as president in succession to Venable, and Stacy as prospective successor to Graham. Chase succeeded Graham and after ten years was drawn away to head the University of Illinois and, later, New York University. Herty and Mills withdrew into commercial chemistry and continued as great pioneers in that field. Wilson went to the University of Chicago in 1932 for ten years of service as dean of the Graduate Library School, returning after retirement there to resume work in the School of Library Science. The remaining five serve the University at the present moment, are the stalwarts in the institution, are the core of that element which gives it tone and has established its place in the intellectual world. They are the peers of the best anywhere. In planning and accomplishment they set standards. By virtue of their presence it was impossible that the University remain provincial.

Venable, of course, does not account for the qualities of these men, but it is an interesting fact that he knew how to select them, apprentice them to the service of letters and science, and hold them here while their qualities were unfolding—and that in a period of extremely low income to the institution and to all who served it. But Venable contributed strongly to the development of faith in the self-generative power of work and striving. An *esprit de corps* founded on will and coordinated purpose came into being under his guidance. The future of the University thus became assured.

Having served the University for twenty years during the poverty of the State (1881-1900) Venable was always over-modest in financial requests after he became president in 1900. He was grounded in the principles of rigid economy, was determined to make every penny count in all expenditures. He kept the strictest accounting and made model financial reports to the trustees for all expenditures and income. He disliked importuning the State for increases, refused the role of lobbyist outright, and held somewhat nearly to the normally impracticable view that it was the business of his office to know his institution, to plan its development in terms of lowest cost, then to set forth these plans in concise terms to the trustees and the legislature. At that point their business began. It was their institution, and investment sense ought to produce the results in income that he had requested. But, unfortunately, appropriations at the hands of a money-granting power are not often strictly on the merits of the case. Political maneuver, the rallying of strategists, the exertion of pressures, and the combination of groups into favoring majority constitute the normal method in attaining desired results. For these things Venable had little or no skill and even less taste. He frankly refused to "hang around" a legislative session, or to delegate such a task to a substitute out of his administrative staff. To Venable's way of thinking such procedure was undignified. The State ought to know its business and see its opportunity after being shown in an honest and formal request. Curiously this process got better results than might be imagined when contrasted with methods in use subsequent to Venable's time. By it State appropriations for the University ran up gradually to a sum four times as great at the end of Venable's administration as it had been at its beginning. True, a rising scale of State income in the fourteen-year period made such a result possible. In view of this and other contributing factors, it is possible that Venable was somewhat too cautious, that he did not always ask for all he might have had. But this presupposes that Venable might have divested himself of his memories of the bitter penury of the State and its University prior to his accession, and his innate distaste for the use of political methods in securing needed funds.

Not only did Venable attain the result of mutiplying the income for maintenance, but he at the same time, with his non-raiding methods and his clear exposition of need as set forth in his reports, brought the State to accept the financial responsibility for a greater expanded plant. Among the first acquisitions was a new chemical laboratory in 1905, at the cost of $50,000, the very first building erected at the University by direct State appropriations. Gone was the old principle and practice, hallowed for over a hundred years, of saying to the University, "we give you permission to live, but you must live on your own, or on your friends." The hitherto stunted child must now have more and better food, not lavish and over-rich to be sure, but an improved diet. Thus science buildings, classroom expansion, and new dormitories for housing the ever-increasing student body came into being at the hands of the State, a State beginning to take pride in its University and sure that its head would suffer no waste.

Venable amply justified this confidence, was a most careful husbandman of the resources placed in his hands, was such a careful spender and apportioner of his funds that many of his staff chafed under the necessary restrictions. Especially was this true of the younger and ambitious men of the faculty now growing up to ever fuller expression of the forces within them. There was never enough money in this place or that to meet the growing needs of any department, old or new, for work tools—books, laboratory room and equipment, assistance by apprentices, class rooms and office rooms—for efficient operation. Each tended to see his own needs and his department's needs for fuller efficiency and to reach by complaint at so narrowly restricted budgets as Venable apportioned. He had to see the whole picture, they naturally saw the limited parts.

Venable, effective as he was in getting the State to take on, for the first time, a frank financial responsibility for its University as its best investment, by no means overlooked or failed to exploit other possible resources of the kind that had enabled it to live, though meagrely, during the long dark years of the State's poverty and its consequent neglect of its University. The tradition was well set and the practice long established of tapping the generosity and favor of friends, patrons, and foundations who could be interested in University needs. Venable never liked to importune for funds, either from the legislature or from private sources. But he was adept at setting before the legislature, in a business-like way, the imperative needs of the institution and then accounting meticulously for every penny received. His financial reports from year to year were models of careful accounting of receipts and disbursements. The state of each endowment fund, great or small, was clearly set forth, showing how it was invested, what returns it had, and how the returns were used. Of course the same was true for appropriations from the State and for receipts from operation. Any interested person whatsoever could resort to his financial reports and gain at any time an exact picture of the material side of the University's life as administered by Venable as a business man.

As already suggested, this distaste for solicitation and political maneuver proved in the end not to have been a bar to increasing generosity at the hands of the State or private donors. Rather it seems to have elevated his person and the institution he headed as worthy of profound respect by virtue of what they were doing, in the State and region, toward widening the bounds of human knowledge and increasing State efficiency. This respect destroyed the old concept, so widely and so long held since the University's reopening in 1875, that the University was an humble pensioner, with hat in hand, seeking merely the right of survival on crumbs.

Hence Venable's period of administration not only saw the State's appropriation for maintenance quadrupled and, in addition, the acceptance by the State of the responsibility for necessary increase in plant and equipment, but also other sources of income opened up of a most important sort in their bearing upon the University's life.

Among these were the beginning of the practice of local alumni associations setting up scholarships to be utilized by students of their choice. This practice in recent years has been allowed to lag, but in its inception and for some years thereafter it exercised an influence of importance in stimulating alumni interest in the University—an interest that is always the healthiest sign of life in an educational institution. The General Education Board assumed responsibility for the salary, a modest one ($2,500), of a professor of secondary education, who was added to the School of Education in the University. Venable's appointee, Nathan Wilson Walker, thereafter for many years devoted his effective talents to intelligent inspection and helpful guidance of the State's high schools and the rapid and healthful expansion of the system. The sum total of Walker's work in this field amounted, in last analysis, to a well coordinated system with uniform standards of organization and curriculum that soon placed the State in the forefront of the regional effort to lift itself out of the educational backwardness that had so long characterized its gestures toward popular education. Walker's work was done so modestly, so free from the fanfare of personal advertisement, that his real achievements have almost escaped the public recognition that has come to other sound contributors to educational advance in the State and the general Southern region. Yet it is not too much to say that this modest and unassuming man, steadfastly supported by the discerning Venable as president of the University, brought order and effectiveness into a high school system that is the capstone of the educational opportunity of the vast majority of the State's citizens. And through it emerges the exceptional element that reaches colleges and universities. This element in Venable's own day fertilized the colleges of the State, and particularly its University in ever increasing numbers, prepared to avail themselves of the opportunity there found to push toward the top of the ladder.

Venable was able to tap the Peabody Fund for resources to erect an education building to house the School of Education; the Carnegie Fund for the new library; other donors were found for book funds to the library, among them the Eugene Armfield Fund for English philology. The McNair Lectures fund was secured, and the Ledoux Fellowship Fund of $5,000 in Venable's beloved chemistry. A private donor gave the Bynum Gymnasium, the first acquisition from any source to promote physical education as a necessary part of a well-rounded educational system. Indeed Venable's patronage and encouragement of college athletics was one of his chief contributions to the University's evolution. He encouraged all sports, but especially had a great liking for football. Yet he was adamant in his purpose and endeavor to keep college athletics in their proper sphere. He recognized the danger of overemphasis, the possibility of encroachment upon the time and interest of serious study and pure intellectual attainment for which a University existed. Amateur athletics were highly desirable and should have a definite, even an important place, in the University scheme; but they should be kept wholly amateur and carefully free from the ills of commercialism and of professional standards.

In these ideas Venable was pitting his strength against an ever-growing trend in most American colleges and universities, a trend which became such a strong current of force that compromise ultimately was the result. Everywhere over the country, within the successive decades of the twentieth century, colleges and universities loomed up as far better known for their athletic prowess than for their intellectual records and standards. Football especially, an enthralling and spectacular game, became an obsession of colleges, and their alumni alike. Money and students poured into not a few institutions, public and private, because of priority, or hope for priority, in athletic reputation. The ever-rising American enthusiasm for sports was capturing the colleges and making them into the main outlet for this impulse. An unknown, but notably large, percentage of young men trooped into the colleges for sports primarily. The amateur principle of college sports was greatly corrupted the country over. Recruiting of promising young athletes by zealous alumni and highly paid coaches became the pattern. Little regard was had for the intellectual qualifications and scholastic preparation of the recruits. Subsidies were provided, sometimes openly, sometimes camouflaged, all to the detriment of intellectual and scholastic standards in the colleges. The colleges yielded to the multiple pressures and suffered the consequences of a lower morale and a partial forgetting of the main objectives of educational institutions. The nadir was reached in the deep South when a demogogic governor in the late twenties, supported by the people of his state, decided to make his state university pre-eminent in athletic renown. Probably the tide since then has been in recession. There is growing evidence that the wounded pride of intellectual idealism is being salved and improvement being affected by the various inter-collegiate councils and conferences built up in recent years to fix and maintain standards of collegiate sports. These are yet somewhere short of perfection, because of the keen competitive spirit and the uneven development among the alumni of the various institutions as to the amount of emphasis college sports should receive.

An over-all defense of the great attention and zealous interest that athletics has received and continues to receive in American colleges and universities rests perhaps more solidly upon the fact that sports make of our country an outdoor people, strong in body and resourceful in all things physical. Our colleges set the style in sports and give the cue to the rest of the youth of the land, inclining them all to a physical purposefulness that is a fundamental asset in peace and in war.

If, in the modern era, England first began to emphasize sports, enabling Wellington to claim that the Battle of Waterloo was won on the cricket fields at Eton, America gradually became the pace-setter in modern outdoor sports, and her influence has affected the rest of the world.

Venable, in his insistence upon purity of standards in college athletics, was not always able to insure against evasions, for he was in a period in which currents ran strong in the competitive race between the colleges for athletic priority, particularly in baseball and football. Public and alumni opinion had not yet seen the danger of overemphasis of athletics on the campuses of the nation throughout, nor had the intercollegiate machinery of councils and conferences yet been built up to regulate standards of practice. But Venable's weight was continually thrown into the scales against abuses of sports. He continually insisted that only unpaid gentlemen, students with good scholastic records, should represent the University in intercollegiate sports. Thereby he laid a tradition in the University's life, a tradition not always since absolutely deferred to, but a tradition nevertheless that has had great weight both in campus and alumni opinion and is still our chief reliance against the pressures that would distort the fundamental purposes of the University's existence.

In another area of influence, also allied closely in Venable's mind with the problem of the correct disciplines he felt necessary to college students in order that they might be trained into self-restrained and orderly minded citizens, he found himself confronted with adverse currents of considerable strength. This was an old problem, not germane to our University alone, but one inherent in most Southern colleges particularly. Hazing new students was in the college tradition, coming down from our English background and literature as a natural part of the conventions of scholastic life. Here it was reinforced by the natural ebullience of youth in a semi-frontier and independent environment. The student body in personnel was quite uneven in social background and, therefore, in social training in the conventions of due respect for individual rights and individual dignity. The incoming college generation was traditionally, then, fair sport for the rough humor and normally mild persecution of other students, particularly for the class one college year ahead. There was much in the air in Venable's period that tended to bulwark the practice, or else to condone it as a feature of college life with useful by-products. These ideas yet held because they were hoary with age and tradition. But Venable believed it high time such tradition were broken. Gentlemen and scholars were not made by rough-house practices of callow youth in derogation of individual dignity. Perhaps he overlooked in some degree the main previous restraint upon the practice—the pronounced tendency of the average North Carolina student to take his own part, to protect his own rights. But this tendency was not within itself sufficiently effective to break down old customs. And in Venable's period occurred at least one tragic episode involving the death, certainly accidental, of a very promising young freshman. Venable took the incident hard, regarding it as a serious reflection upon his administration and a blot upon the growing fair name of the University. He planned and carried through a careful and thorough investigation with the idea of drastic punishment for all students involved in the incident. A special faculty committee was set up for the investigation, himself presiding. He exhausted himself over the details. Immediate outcome was dismissal from the University of a few students who were closest in on the affair. Ultimate outcome was a sobering of student opinion on the problem of hazing and the ripening of a conviction among students themselves that the practice had no place in an institution of learning now rapidly growing to adulthood.

Student discipline had hitherto always been a duty and responsibility of the president and the faculty, definitely placed upon their shoulders by trustee regulations. For the exercise of this responsibility there existed a committee in the faculty, called "The Executive Committee," but having to do only with matters of breach of good citizenship in student conduct. This committee, whose work was never pleasant or agreeable, was, in Venable's administration, developing the conviction that good college citizenship could best be secured by involving the student body itself in student government. Direct transition to student self-government was held to be too drastic a change. Venable himself distrusted it as a very doubtful risk. But he agreed that good might come from an association of student machinery with that of the faculty for the common purpose of good student government. Hence a Students' Council came into being, made up of the presidents of the three classes above the freshman class plus the presidents of the upper classes in the Schools of Law, Pharmacy, and Medicine. These were all elective officers, filled by majority of student votes. In addition there was one further representative on the Council chosen from the Senior class by the Council itself.

The authority of this Council was delegated authority, informally transferred by the faculty itself and encouraged and stabilized by the faculty as a promising experiment in democratic government and citizenship training. The Council was not intended to have full and complete jurisdiction, except where acquiesced in by the president and faculty Executive Committee.

At first the new machinery of a Students' Council concerned itself largely with infractions of the Honor System. This system had been slowly growing up as an expression of student sentiment that it should be a student responsibility to insure against dishonesty in examinations and all written work. The system was slow in making entire conquest of student support. It ran strongly against the grain, particularly in the two lower academic classes, for a student to charge one of his fellows. This seemed to be an inherent aversion, coming up from small-boy days. Nevertheless it was easier for the average student to report infractions to a Students' Council than to a Faculty Committee. He felt that the Council was his own, composed of his own immediate representatives, and would be more understanding, probably less impersonal than a faculty group. The point was important in the students' concept.

Yet the transition to full authority of the Council in the maintenance and development of the Honor System was difficult to make by reason of several obstacles. One was the obvious tendency of the Council to levy lighter penalties for infractions, penalties that the faculty, or at least many of its members, held to be inadequate. Another reason for the slow extension of Council jurisdiction was the reluctance of the faculty members to turn over cases to the Council which they individually uncovered as infractions of the Honor System. They preferred reporting them to the faculty Executive Committee according to established custom. There was much good reason for this attitude beside the generally lighter penalties levied by the Council in case of conviction. The best reason perhaps was the fact that the Council, by virtue of its composition of students, was not generally qualified to weigh internal evidence, which was often the main evidence of dishonesty in an examination paper. Judgment of such evidence often required a broader, and sometimes a more detailed knowledge of the subject matter than the student judges could have been expected to possess. Simple cases, where one or several students reported to the Council that they saw an individual directly "cribbing" the work of another, made procedure and results of Council action fairly effective. But where proof of a more complicated sort was a basis of the action the matter was more difficult and miscarriage of justice more likely.

Nevertheless, despite overlapping jurisdiction, there was a fairly healthy growth of Council effectiveness. It did not bring in a golden millennium, and has not to this day. But it did strengthen student morale somewhat, and superinduced pride in "Carolina Honor" as guarded by a democratic system of self-government. Other matters of conduct not beseeming gentlemen and good college citizenship gradually became subjects of Council cognizance. The social effects and implications of liquor drinking among students has always been a knotty problem at Carolina, as perhaps in most American educational institutions. For long years the burden was upon the administration and the faculty to hold this tendency in check. A special State law had long since erected Chapel Hill and its immediate vicinity into a prohibition area and, though never since repealed, its effect upon the circulation of liquor was quite similar to American experience under the late "noble experiment" of the Volstead Act.

Also, special trustee legislation sought to bulwark prohibition of student drinking. By trustee direction and a standing order, there was annually printed in the college catalogue the statement that the faculty was required to "dismiss from the University any student known to engage in drinking intoxicating liquor." This Draconian law was evidently not intended to be elastic, but in the nature of the case its application had to be. The faculty placed the burden of execution upon the Executive Committee, while both itself and the committee was made up ordinarily of men of unequal degrees of tolerance of the drink evil. Result was, and naturally, that only outstanding or outrageous abuses were dealt with under the probably too drastic law.

When the Council began to grow up in Venable's time and to seek to expand its jurisdiction, the matter of drinking was one of the earliest to be taken under purview. Explanation of this trend lay in the fact of a different code among students than that represented in the Trustee law. The students' code was more practical, extending only to grave excesses and public display of such excesses. It had a chance of real enforcement, on the basis of ripening student sentiment that excesses of any sort were socially demeaning. This ripening of sentiment was not over-fast. Year to year, changing of the personnel of the Council produced variability of attitude in enforcement, leaving it an open question whether the democratic process would work out a permanent advance. The age level of the average student and the consequent immaturity posed the issue of the workability of relaxing faculty control. Venable, as responsible head of the institution, while he hoped for good to come out of the experiment and encouraged the development, was on the conservative side and leaned strongly to the principle that final authority must continue to rest with the faculty in cases where effective results were not forthcoming from the Students' Council. Nor would he have the student body forget this point. This is the explanation of the fact, or much of it, that Venable's administration left in students' minds the impression of illiberality, of emphasis upon discipline and authority. Even portions of his faculty shared in this concept, without correctly evaluating the seriousness with which he took his responsibilities and the necessities therefor.

Yet by the time this administration had closed, North Carolina had a notably more liberal and distinctive University on every level of internal organization and external projections. Internally the Honor System was healthy though the puerilities of hazing were not yet extinct, and ideals of good college citizenship had been greatly advanced. Students were coming up to the University in greatly enlarged numbers and finding there an organism seriously committed to preparing men for the work of life. The material University, the faculty, and the curriculum all had been greatly expanded to this end. Only some notable cataclysm of social and economic disaster would threaten progress toward the goal of national distinction and usefulness.

Venable was in no sense a dashing or spectacular person. Innately modest, he distrusted some of his own powers and was not wholly at ease on a public platform, a position most college presidents enjoy and find an effective medium for their influence. It might even be said with truth that platform artistry constitutes much of the equipment of not a few college presidents. Venable spoke well and to the point, even though without special grace and ease. He talked sense without flourishes or any labored effort for ornate effect. He was a scientist first and foremost and accepted himself as such. He was an administrator next and he hoped to succeed in this role by the use of common sense, by long familiarity with the needs of his particular institution, and by an equally long apprenticeship to them as professor before he became president. He was sincere to the core and without artifice in any of his acts. His gift of humor was not great, though he appreciated this quality in others. Small talk was not his forte, yet he was thoroughly at ease in social relations. Never ebullient and always possessed of natural personal dignity, he nevertheless gave the impression of friendliness and concern about others. Familarity or excess of informality were wholly absent from his concept of personal relations among gentlemen. He was not socially subtle-minded and took no occasion to make that impression. To more supple-minded persons he seemed a bit austere, but his gravity was that of the intense scientist or the overworked administrator. He was a good churchman in the Presbyterian communion, accepting cheerfully all the obligations of service that fell to him in that church as first a prominent professor in the village and then president of the University. But no bigotry whatever tinged his attitude in matters of creed and church affiliation. He had the toleration of the true scientist and believed that the gradual unfolding of the human intellect, prompted by individual effort, would bring man around to a balanced and disciplined life. Self-discipline was the true means of attaining an orderly life but, where this fell short in youth or undeveloped citizens, Venable held for external restraints justly applied in the social interest. And, despite much modern experimentation and trial of new theories about the training of youth, "training" remains a basic idea. Training implies discipline in its very nature. Where this discipline may be self-evolved or evoked, so much better is the training. Where it stops short, or fails to function, social obligation steps in to assist, to encourage, to guide, and, where necessary, to restrain.

Venable in his earlier years, especially before he became overburdened with administration duties and the amount of teaching that he insisted on retaining in chemistry, had a strong spirit of play. He loved tennis especially and played a good game. He encouraged and assisted the beginning of a golf interest among the faculty and the origin of a very limited golf course, first of two holes and finally of five, before the later transfer of site and expansion in later years.

Venable was the punctiliously correct gentleman in his home life, had the great advantage of a loyal and intelligent wife, Sallie Manning, daughter of John Manning, head of the University Law School from 1881 to his death in 1899. To the pair (married in 1884) a family of five children had been born, in succession two daughters, twin sons, and a third daughter. Venable greatly interested himself in the training, education, and development of his well-balanced family, was a disciplinarian without harshness, and altogether a model husband and father.

In physical aspects Venable was tall, erect, and possessed of a strong frame that gave the impression of some angularity without detracting from his general appearance as a well-set-up figure. He had a broad and high brow, prominent cheek bones, and a very firm chin. His eyes were blue-gray, direct, and piercing. He wore a full beard in his earlier years at the University, when full hirsutes were fashionable. Later he compromised on a moustache which he retained the remainder of his life.

Beginning with the summer of 1913 President Venable, worn with his heavy tasks of administration, was granted a leave of absence by the Board of Trustees to recuperate his strength. Full pay ($4,000, the then presidential salary) was voted, this against Venable's advice. He stated that he did not wish to be an additional expense to the University's slender resources. However, his view did not prevail, the relief being clearly his due. In further care of University interest Venable pointed out in his request for leave that the burdens of the office as then concentrated in the president were too heavy for one man to bear, and requested the body to consider methods by which some part of the duties of the office might be reduced. This answers the point of criticism of some of Venable's contemporaries that he loved the feel of power, that he knew little about how to delegate functions to subordinates, that he personally liked to cover an unduly large area of activities.

True perspective discloses the fact that Venable had, in 1900, come to the administrative headship of a small college. By 1913 this small college, still very much undernourished financially, had grown into a University. Venable had had to make every penny count and had chosen to pinch on administrative machinery and personnel, always emphasizing to the trustees and the legislature the need of expenditures for buildings, laboratories, and teaching staff. The remarkable growth of the University in the latter aspects was almost wholly unaccompanied by any corresponding growth in administrative machinery and administrative personnel. Venable personally absorbed the additional burdens that came with the expansion of student numbers, of the teaching staff, and the greatly expanded physical plant. Thus he became the victim of the University's growth, subjecting himself to ever-increasing strain that would have broken a less vigorous and forceful man earlier. This course was quite in keeping with the self-sacrificing quality of the man. If the University could grow and fulfill its high functions, what mattered the burdens he himself bore? In this attitude he was probably unwise, since the expansion of administrative machinery was clearly indicated as a primary need in the face of a greatly expanded institution. But, confident in his own strength and over-generous with his energies, he drove forward under ever-increasing burdens until it was too late to save himself from shattered nerves.

Since Venable's day administrative machinery has been constantly multiplied until it has caught up to, if not lately outrun, the needs of the University. We have turned a full cycle. Then the source of administrative decisions was easy to find. This source was Venable, giving ground for the criticism of some. Now, without a change of theory as to the functions of the presidency, the problem is to find your way around in the maze of administrative machinery and reach a source where final decisions may be had.

The same trustee meeting, June 3, 1913, that granted Venable leave, by his recommendation elected Edward Kidder Graham as acting president for the succeeding year, assigning him the regular presidential salary.

Venable soon thereafter sailed for Europe, a custom as ingrained in American intellectuals as it was in American socialites and other pleasure seekers. This was part and parcel of national habit, the deference paid to an old society and the home of our race, as well as to the accumulated values of occidental culture and science. Venable, primarily a scientist, apparently planned to use his leave for renewal of his contacts with the scientific world, particularly that part of it represented by Germany. Germans for a number of decades past had been setting the pace in the sciences, particularly in chemistry, Venable's great passion. It was now some thirty years since he had attained degrees at Göttingen and attended lectures on science at the University of Berlin. Now he planned no consistent study, but looked forward to relaxation in a congenial scientific environment.

Unfortunately or fortunately—for Venable—his health did not improve as had been expected. He wrote from London to the trustees, May 7, 1914, that the condition of his health, as advised by his physicians, would not permit him to resume the presidency upon the expiry of his leave. He therefore tendered his resignation. The Board of Trustees, May 28, at its regular early summer meeting, accepted his resignation with appropriate expressions of regret and on the same day created the Francis Preston Venable Chair of Chemistry and forthwith elected Venable to fill it. Thus was retired, from administrative responsibility for an actual University, a man who had borne burdens so heavy that only an iron man could have sustained them for a great length of time.

Edward Kidder Graham, immediately elected president, was young and fresh, filled with confidence and a great zeal. Yet he sustained the burden for only four years before exhaustion and death. This, too, when his first three years had the stimulus of new adjustments hailed by the old critics of Venable as a regeneration. Graham's last year, coterminous with our World War effort, saw the war as a precipitant to close-haul the forces and spirit of the University, faculty, students, and administration, to the one aim of meeting the great threat to national safety. Underneath seeming surface confusion one principle was moving, one current drawing, that of fitting the University and its whole personnel to contribute effectively to the national purpose of victory.

Venable's retirement from the presidency was therefore practically coterminous with the end of an era. Always strained to the limit of his endurance he handed on the University to other hands barely in time to save his life. The swirling forces of the succeeding era would have overborne him entirely. Though he continued to live and prove effective in his chair of chemistry, it was with the nub of his strength in a period so fraught with change for the country that there was little time for contemporary evaluation of his great services. So modest was he by nature, however, he never seemed aware that the usual acclaim bestowed by the public upon those who "richly deserve" was in any way absent. Seemingly he knew no slight was intended, no time allowable for retrospect. More probably still, he was too modest, too self-effacing to assume that his career of service gave him any title to adulation. Not even early death came to his aid. He lived on into a growing weakness until mental eclipse darkened his last years and a new generation had arisen. This generation was preoccupied with the present, not with the past, when Venable passed on in 1934, the very shell of the man who had wrought so generously for the University. If acclaim was lacking then, compensation lay in the fact that he had never listened for acclaim and applause.

INDEX

Academies, role in education in N. C., 32, 32 n.
Agrarian movement, leaders of, fight for establishment of agricultural and mechanical college, 39, 43, 44 ff. *See also* Populist party
Agricultural and Mechanical College. *See* North Carolina State College of Agriculture and Engineering
Agriculture, taught at University, 19, 20, 45-46; Battle's attitude toward, 46; State College's contributions to, 48; in N. C. at turn of century, 81
Alderman, Edwin Anderson, 66-76; as leader in popular education movement, 58, 61-62, 66, 67 ff. *passim*, 71-72, 75; qualifications for presidency of University, 62, 74, 74-75, 79; taste and manners of, 66-67, 73; as skilled speaker, 69, 73-74; fights for University in church-state controversy over higher education, 72, 75; contributions to University, 72-74, 80; resigns presidency of University, 77; mentioned, 49, 58, 78, 87
Alderman, Susan Cobbett, 66
Alexander, Eben, sketch of, 55; mentioned, 51, 53, 85, 86, 88
Alumni, aid Battle in fight for state support to University, 41; donations from during Battle's administration, 49-50; establish University scholarships, 92
Alumni Association, revived under Battle, 39
Ansonian, The, 44
Anti-Federalists, fear power of State University, 7-8
Armfield Fund, 93
Athletics, emphasis upon in colleges and universities, 38, 93 ff.; Venable's attitude toward, 85, 93, 94-95, 101
Atkins, General Smith B., 13
Aycock, Charles Brantley, contributions to popular education movement, 67, 68, 81-82

Badger, George E., 28
Bailey, Josiah W., in church-state controversy over higher education, 40, 60, 61, 75, 80, 87

Bain, Charles W., 88
Baptists, 18, 21. *See also* Churches
Battle, Elisha, 27
Battle, Kemp Plummer, 23-50; role in reopening of University, 18, 19-20; leads University in policy of political moderation, 21, 25-26, 30-31, 49; policy on religious affiliation of Faculty members, 21, 43; particularly suited for presidency of reopened University, 24-25, 30-31; political complexion of, 25-26, 28-29; family background of, 27-28; career before becoming president of University, 28-29; sketch of, 30; accomplishments of administration of, 34 ff., 80; fights for state funds for University, 39-43 *passim;* efforts to retain Land Scrip Fund for University, 45 ff.; "head and hand" concept of agricultural education, 46; retires from presidency, 49; fills University chair of history, 51; mentioned, 67, 72, 74, 75, 78, 85, 86, 87
Battle, Richard Horn, Jr., 28
Battle, William Horn, career of, 28; heads Law School in reopened University, 34-35; mentioned, 18
Battle family, characteristics, 27
Beaufort, N. C., work in marine biology at, 59
Bequests to University. *See* Gifts
Biblical Recorder, 21, 40, 42, 60
Bingham's School, 32 n.
Blair, J. J., contributions to popular education movement, 69
Board and room, in 1875, 20
Board of Trustees, and opening of University, 6-7; political leanings of early members of, 7, 9; selection of University presidents by, 9, 24-25, 25 n., 74, 77, 103; during Reconstruction, 15; role in reopening of University, 18 ff.; reorganize University, 1875, 20; aid Battle in fight for state support of University, 41; seek to control student drinking, 98; and Venable's resignation, 103
Bourbons, overthrown by Populists, 76
Brann, William Cowper, 63
Brogden, Governor C. H., 35

105

Bryan, William J., 75
Bynum Gymnasium, 93

Cain, William, sketch of, 53-55; mentioned, 51, 53, 85, 86
Caldwell, Joseph, first term as president of University, 9; second administration of, 10; mentioned, 16, 21
Caldwell, Tod R., attitude toward reopening of University, 18
Cameron, Paul C., 18, 50
Carnegie, Andrew, 37, 38, 83
Carnegie Fund, 93
Carnegie Library, at University, 37-38, 83
Carter, D. M., role in reopening of University, 18, 19
Chapman, Robert Hett, 9
Chartering Act, 6
Chase, Harry Woodburn, 88
"Christian Education *versus* Godless Education," 40-41, 60-61
Christian Educator, 40, 61
Churches, oppose state support to University, 39-43, 47-48, 60 ff., 72, 75, 87; fight for clerical control of higher education, 40-41, 60 ff.
Civil War, effect of upon University, 12-13
Coates, Albert, 36
Cobb, Collier, conducts geology summer school at King's Mountain, 59; mentioned, 74, 85, 86
Coeducation, attitude toward in 1890's, 69-70
Coker, Robert Erwin, 56 n.
Coker, William Chambers, 88, 89
Common school system. *See* Popular education movement
Conduct. *See under* Students
Consolidation, 47, 53-54, 69
Constitution of N. C., first, provides for establishment of University, 5-6; of 1868, 15, 18
Craig, Locke, 67
Craven, Braxton, 40
Crowell, John F., 40
Curriculum of University, after reopening, 20; effect of Land Scrip Fund upon, 19, 20, 45-46; reorganized by Venable, 84
Curry, J. L. M., 68

Dancy, Frank B., 67

Davidson College, 40, 41
Davie, William R., as father of University, 9
Deems Fund, 36-37
Democratic party, control in N. C., 16, 17, 21, 25, 26; University allegiance to after reopening, 21-22; and Bryan's monetary reform program, 75-76; Bourbon influence in, 76; lose control to Fusionists, 25 n., 60, 76
Denominational controversy. *See* Churches
Dey, William Morton, 88, 89
Dialectic Society, 11
Discipline. *See under* Students
Donations to University. *See* Gifts
Drinking, control of at University, 98-99
Duke family, financial patronage given to Trinity College, 60, 61, 62
Duke University, present position of, 62. *See also* Trinity College
Durham, Columbus, 40

Education in N. C., in colonial days, 3 ff.; contributions of academies to, 32, 32 n.; Negro, 35; church-state controversy over, 39-43, 47-48, 60 ff., 72, 75, 87; of women, 69 ff. *See also* Popular education movement, University of North Carolina
Elisha Mitchell Scientific Society, 78
Endowment of University. *See* University of North Carolina, gifts to *and* state support of
Engineering School, transferred from University to State College, 47, 53-54
Enrollment, at date of first Commencement, 7; during Caldwell's administration, 10; during Swain's administration, 10-11, 13; in 1875, 24; during Battle's administration, 31 n., 39, 49; during Winston's administration, 57, 59 n.; during Venable's administration, 82
Episcopal Church, alleged influence upon University, 43
Escheats, given to University, 6
Eugene Armfield Fund, 93

Faculty, in early days of University, 7, 8; in 1875, 20-21; tradition that members refrain from participation in politics, 22; during Battle's admin-

istration, 39, 43, 67; of the 1890's, 51-56; and student discipline, 52, 53, 96 ff. *passim;* at time of Alderman's inauguration, 74-75; under Venable, 85-89, 90-91; Executive Committee of, 96 ff. *passim*
Farmers Association, 45
Federalist party, influence upon University, 7-8, 33 n. *See also* Whig party
Fellowships, established during Venable's administration, 93
Football, exploitation of on American campuses, 93-94
Francis Preston Venable Chair of Chemistry, 103
Fusionists, gain control of N. C., 25 n., 60, 76

Gales, Seaton, 18
General Assembly, charters University, 6; elects Board of Trustees for University, 18; restores Land Scrip Fund to University, 19; establishes Woman's College at Greensboro, 69, 71. *For appropriations made to University, see* University of North Carolina, state support of
General Education Board, pays salary of professor of secondary education at University, 92
Geology Department, 59
Geology summer school, 59
Gerrard Hall, defaced by students during Winston's administration, 63-64
Gifts to University, encouraged in Chartering Act, 6; enabling reopening after Reconstruction, 19-20; during Battle's administration, 36-37, 49-50; during Venable's administration, 37-38, 83, 92 ff.
Gillaspie, J. S., 8
"Godless education *versus* Godly education," 40-41, 60-61
Golf, 101
Gore, Joshua W., 51, 85, 86
Graduate school, established, 84
Graham, Alexander, and popular education movement, 58, 69
Graham, Edward Kidder, as president of University, 103-4; mentioned, 88
Graham, W. A., service to University, 19, 23; public career of, 23 n.; mentioned, 17, 18, 28
Graves, Ralph H., 20, 21, 67

Hamilton, J. G. deRoulhac, 88, 89
Harrington, Carl P., 51
Harris, Charles Wilson, 7, 8
Harris, Dr. Thomas, conducts medical school at University, 36
Hazing, at University, 95-96
Henderson, Archibald, 88, 89
Herty, Charles Holmes, 88
Hill Music Hall, 39
Holden, W. W., impeachment of, 15, 16; mentioned, 18
Holmes, Joseph A., 51
Holt, J. Allen, 32 n.
Honor system, beginnings of, 1875, 20; development of at University, 97-98
Hooper, J. De B., 20
Horner, J. Hunter, 32 n.
Horner's School, 32 n.
Howe, George, 88
Hume, Thomas, sketch of, 52-53; mentioned, 43, 85, 86

Iconoclast, The, 63
Institute of Government, 36
Institutes. *See* Academies *and* Teachers institutes

James, Hinton, 7
Jarvis, Governor T. J., champions state support of University, 42; mentioned, 35
Johns Hopkins, as new force in higher education, 56
Joyner, James Y., contributions to popular education movement, 67, 69, 71

Ker, David, 7, 8
Kilgo, J. C., role in church-state controversy over higher education, 40-41, 60-62, 75, 80, 87
Kimberly, John, 20
King's Mountain, N. C., geology summer school conducted at, 59
Ku Klux Klan, 15, 16

Land Grant Fund. *See* Land Scrip Fund
Land Scrip Fund, secured by Swain for University, 14; restored to University after reopening, 19; effect upon University curriculum, 19, 20, 45-46; amount of, 39; sought by advocates of separate agricultural and mechanical college, 39, 43 ff.; University

loses to A. & M. College, 47; effect of removal of upon development of University, 70; mentioned, 26
Latta, James E., 88
Law, study of in ante-bellum N. C., 34
Law School, reopened after Civil War, 34-35; summer session established during Winston's administration, 58-59
Ledoux Fellowship Fund, 93
Lee, Robert E., 24 n.
Legislature. *See* General Assembly
Library resources, improved by Winston, 59; Alderman's contributions to improvement of, 72-73; growth in concept of need for, 82, 83; expansion program during Venable's administration, 82-84, 93. *For library buildings, see* Carnegie Library, University Library

McGehee, Lucius Polk, 88
McIver, Charles D., contributions to popular education movement, 67 ff. *passim;* leads movement for education of women, 69 ff.; service to Woman's College, 71; mentioned, 49, 58
McNair Lectures, 93
MacNider, W. de B., 88, 89
Malone, Dumas, on Edwin Anderson Alderman, 66, 66 n., 72
Mangum, A. W., 20, 21
Mangum, Willie P., 28
Manly, Charles, 18
Manning, John, 34, 51, 58, 101
Manufacturing, in N. C., 81
Marine biology summer school, 59
Mebane, C. H., in church-state controversy over higher education, 61
Mechanic arts, in curriculum of University, 19, 20, 45-46
Medical School, beginnings of, 1879-85, 36
Memorial Hall (old), history of, 49-50
Methodists, 18, 21. *See also* Churches
Mills, J. E., 88
Moore, B. F., 17, 18
Moses, Edward P., contributions to popular education movement, 68, 69
Museum, of early University, 7

Negro, normal school, 35; as political issue during Bourbon regime, 76

Noble, M. C. S., contributions to popular education movement, 67, 69; mentioned, 58, 85, 86
Normal school, for Negroes, 35. *See also* Summer normal school
North Carolina, Whig régime in, 10; during Reconstruction, 15, 16; Democratic party control in, 16, 17, 21, 25, 26; Fusionist control of, 25 n., 60, 76; signs of economic rehabilitation at turn of century, 81. *See also* Constitution of N. C.; Education in N. C.; University of N. C., state support of
North Carolina State College of Agriculture and Engineering, agrarian leaders fight to establish, 39 ff.; and Consolidation, 47, 53-54; contributions to industry and agriculture in N. C., 48; changes in name of, 53 n.; under G. T. Winston, 64; mentioned, 70
North Carolina Teachers Association, 35

Oak Ridge Academy, 32 n.

Page, Walter H., 57
Patterson, A. H., 88
Patterson, Rufus, 18
Peabody Hall, 93
Peabody Fund, 93
Pharmacy School, 36
Philanthropic Society, 11
Philanthropy, and educational institutions, 37-39
Phillips, Charles, position in Faculty of 1875, 20-21, 23-24
Phillips, James, career of, 16
Polk, L. L., fights for establishment of separate A. & M. college, 43, 44 ff.; career of, 44
Pool, Solomon, 15
Popular education movement, University's role in, 31-32, 57-58, 61-62, 71-72, 75, 92-93; leaders of, 49, 58, 67-69, 81-82
Populist party, fusion between Republican party and, 25 n., 60, 76
Presbyterian church, influence upon early University, 18, 21; attitude toward state support of University, 40, 41
Progressive Farmer, The, 44

INDEX

Public education. *See* Popular education movement

Public school system, development after Reconstruction, 31, 31 n. *For University's contributions to, see* Popular education movement, Summer normal school

Reconstruction, and the University, 13-14, 15 ff.; in N. C., 15, 16

Record. See *University Record*

Redd, A. F., 20, 21

Republican party, and the University, 9, 15, 26, 60; and Reconstruction in N. C., 15, 16; fusion between Populist party and, 25 n., 60, 76

Room and board, in 1875, 20

Salaries, Faculty, cut during Battle's administration, 39; Winston's, 63; of professor of secondary education (during Venable's administration), 92; Venable's, 101

Saunders, W. L., 18, 50

Scholarships, 92

School of Education, 92, 93

Science, evolution of school of at University, 47; Henry Van Peter Wilson's contributions to, 56; prominence in University at time of Alderman's inauguration, 74; Venable's contributions to, 77-78, 80

Secondary education professorship, established at University, 92

Sectarian controversy. See Churches

Shepherd, James E., 59

Sherman, General W. T., 15

Smith, Charles Alphonso, 88

Spencer, Cornelia Phillips, and the University, 16 ff., 19, 85-86; mentioned, 23, 29

Stacy, Marvin Hendrix, 88

State College. *See* North Carolina State College of Agriculture and Engineering

State Normal and Industrial School. *See* Woman's College

State support of University. *See* University of North Carolina, state support of

State universities, not favored by philanthropists, 37

Steele, Walter Leak, 18, 50

Student aid, 36-37

Student Government. *See* Students' Council

Students, response to war, 12; conduct and discipline of: in the 1890's, 52, 53, during Winston's administration, 63-64, during Venable's administration, 84-85, 95 ff.; and hazing, 95-96; and drinking, 98-99. *See also* Enrollment *and* Students' Council

Students' Council, beginnings of, 1875, 20; development and activities during Venable's administration, 96 ff.

Summer normal school, instituted during Battle's administration, 35; University loses state appropriation for, 35-36, 43, 58; revived during Winston's administration, 58, 72

Summer schools, set up during Winston's administration, 58-59

Swain, David Lowrie, 10-14; accomplishments as president of University, 10-11, 14; political complexion of, 10-14 *passim;* unpopularity after Civil War, 13-14; death of, 15; mentioned, 21, 26, 32

Swain, Eleanor, marriage of, 13

Taylor, C. E., in church-state controversy over higher education, 60

Teachers, University's work in training, 35-36, 57-58, 71-72; role of, 86. *See also* Teachers institutes *and* Woman's College

Teachers institutes, leaders of, 69; as part of popular education movement, 68-69

Tenant farming, 48

Toy, Walter Dallam, 43, 51

Trinity College, and church-state controversy over higher education, 40, 60, 61; receives patronage of Duke family, 60, 61, 62. *See also* Duke University

Trustees. *See* Board of Trustees

Trusts, and church-state controversy over higher education, 61

Tuition at University, in 1875, 20; free: provisions for, 6, 39, 42, 49, church opposition to, 40, 42, 42 n.

University Library, 83

University of North Carolina, established, 5-6; state support of: limited provision for in Chartering Act, 6, obtained by Swain, 14, during Battle's administration, 35-36, 42-43, 44, during Winston's administration, 59, during Venable's administration, 80-81, 82, 90, 91-92, during Alderman's administration, 81, church opposition to, 39-43, 47-48, 60 ff., 72, 75, 87; gifts to, 6, 19-20, 36-39, 49-50, 83, 92 ff.; opening of, 7; political influences affecting: Anti-Federalist, 7 ff. *passim,* Federalist, 7 ff. *passim,* 33 n., Republican, 9, 15, 26, 60, Whig, 10 ff. *passim,* 25, 33 n., Democratic, 21-22, Populist, 60; under Robert Hett Chapman, 9; under Caldwell, 9, 10; under Swain, 10-14; academic standing of: before Civil War, 11, 12, under Battle, 31, 32, at time of Alderman's inauguration, 74, under Venable, 87-88; sectional feeling at, 12, 33; and the Land Scrip Fund, 14, 19, 39, 43 ff., 47, 70; closed after Civil War, 15-16; during Reconstruction, 15 ff., 29; fight to reopen, 17 ff.; religious influences upon: Presbyterian, 18, 21, 41, Episcopal, 43, *see also* Churches; reopening of, 19-20, 24; under Battle, 21, 25-26, 30-32, 34-50, 80; contributions to popular education, 31-32, 57-58, 61-62, 71-72, 75, 92-93; prestige of in N. C., 32-33; and Consolidation, 47, 53-54, 69; under Winston, 51-65, 80; under Alderman, 66-76, 80; under Venable, 77-104. *See also* Board of Trustees, Curriculum, Enrollment, Faculty, *and* Students

University of North Carolina Press, 78

University of Texas, during George T. Winston's administration, 62 ff.

University Press, established by Venable, 78

University Record, importance of, 75 n., 78

Vance, Zebulon B., role in reopening of University, 19; mentioned, 17, 35

Venable, Charles Scott, 77

Venable, Francis Preston, 77-104; service to University before becoming president, 53, 77 ff.; scientific achievements of, 77-78, 80; as an administrator, 79-80, 84 ff., 100, 102; achievements as president, 79-84, 88, 89, 90, 92, 99, 102; financial policies of, 80-81, 82, 89 ff.; attitude toward athletics, 85, 93, 94-95, 101; stand on hazing, 95-96; as speaker, 99-100; sketch of, 99 ff.; granted leave of absence, 101-2; resigns presidency, 103; last days of, 104; mentioned, 51, 67, 74

Venable, Sallie Manning, 101

Virginia, 77

Wake Forest College, 40, 60, 61, 62

Walker, Nathan Wilson, 88

Whig party, régime in N. C., 10; influence on University, 10 ff. *passim,* 25, 33 n.; post-Civil War policy of, 13-14; absorbed into Democratic party, 16, 17, 21, 26

Whitehead, R. H., 51, 85, 86

Williams, Horace, 51

Wilson, Henry Van Peters, sketch of, 55-57; conducts summer school in marine biology, 59; mentioned, 51, 53, 74, 78, 85, 86

Wilson, Louis R., library work of, 83-84, 88-89; mentioned, 82, 88

Winston, George Tayloe, 51-65; service to University before becoming president, 20, 21, 41-42, 51; as ideal choice for president of University, 57, 78, 79; contributions to popular education, 57-58, 61-62; accomplishments of administration of, 57 ff., 80; fights denominational opposition to University, 60 ff., 72, 75, 80; as president of University of Texas, 62 ff.; arbitrary tendencies of, 63-64; after retirement from public life, 64-65; mentioned, 67, 71, 74, 75, 78, 87

Winston, R. W., 67

Winston's "Military Academy," 63-64

Woman's College of the University of North Carolina, founded, 69, 71; McIver's role in establishing, 71; mentioned, 47, 54

Women, education of. *See under* Education

World War I, student response to, 12

www.ingramcontent.com/pod-product-compliance
Lightning Source LLC
Chambersburg PA
CBHW030117010526
44116CB00005B/294